It is vital that we recover the practice
Biblical principles, pastoral encourage
us. May it be widely used to help paren
in the ways of the Lord and ultimately

Bill James
Principal, London Seminary

Corporate worship in the church should be the overflow of family worship at home. Terry Johnson has provided a biblical yet practical resource to encourage family times together around the throne of grace. This book will help you to deepen your understanding or sharpen your practice of family worship, Read it! Use it! Share it!

H. B. Charles Jr.
Pastor-teacher, Shiloh Metropolitan Baptist Church, Jacksonville, Florida
Speaker and author of several books

I learn something from Terry Johnson about historic Christian worship (whether public, private or family) every time I read him. This book (a wonderful companion to my well-worn copy of his *Family Worship Book*) is not only a practical help to families seeking to strengthen (or begin) their practice of family devotions, but has multiple other uses and applications. It is something that I will use with those preparing for the ministry. Its rich devotional and historical theological insights have already blessed me as I read it myself.

Ligon Duncan
Chancellor and CEO, Reformed Theological Seminary

Family worship is arguably the most neglected biblical duty of Christian parents today. Terry Johnson demonstrates the biblical and practical necessity of family worship. He also gives both encouragement and a guide for practicing it. This is a short book, but has long term consequences for you and your family. Get it and read it. Then get on your knees and pray for strength to put it into practice.

Bill Barcley
Senior Pastor, Sovereign Grace Presbyterian Church Charlotte,
North Carolina
Adjunct Professor of New Testament, Reformed Theological Seminary

...This book comes at just the right time and as just the right medicine. I run out of adjectives to commend it: Clear, concise, and compelling, it grips the soul with a divine imperative and yet, warms the heart with the friendly touch of a father's hand upon the shoulder. I feel sure my family shall be very much the better for its arrival, and yours can be too if you will but read, mark, learn, and practically apply its truth to your most precious of all possessions – your family. Dr. Johnson has done us all a tremendous service.

Neil Stewart
Pastor, Christ Covenant Church, Greensboro, North Carolina

Christian parents long to see their children grow up to be whole-life disciples of Jesus. However, a lot of us are not sure what we should be doing in order to help our children mature spiritually. We can see the problem clearly: busyness, distraction, and all of the temptations of the devil, world, and flesh. What we're uncertain about is the solution. This book taps into deep streams of biblical and traditional wisdom in order to show parents how a recovery of family worship is perhaps the most important thing that we can be doing in order to raise our children as disciples of Jesus. Any parent who feels confused about what it means to 'bring them up in the training and admonition of the Lord' (Eph. 6:4) needs to read this book.

Joe Barnard
Pastor, Holyrood Evangelical Church, Edinburgh
Author of *The Way Forward* and *Surviving the Trenches*

This book paints a beautiful portrait of our glorious heritage in the Reformed tradition. The church in the twenty-first century desperately needs to be convicted, challenged, and encouraged by our faithful forefathers of the past. In this book, Dr. Terry Johnson helps to unearth the treasure trove of precious truths from our past to the end that we might know better how to live as becomes the followers of Jesus Christ today. This resource is not only for families—it is for every Christian, younger or older, who humbly desires to grow in his or her communion with and adoration of our triune Lord.

Burk Parsons
Senior Pastor, Saint Andrew's Chapel, Sanford, Florida
Editor of Tabletalk Magazine

UNDERSTANDING FAMILY WORSHIP

Its History, Theology and Practice

TERRY L. JOHNSON

CHRISTIAN
FOCUS

Scripture quotations are from *The Holy Bible, English Standard Version*, copyright © 2001 by Crossway Bibles, a publishing ministry of Good News Publishers. Used by permission. All rights reserved. ESV Text Edition: 2011.

Copyright © Terry L. Johnson 2022

paperback ISBN 978-1-5271-0788-5
ebook ISBN 978-1-5271-0862-2

Published in 2022
by
Christian Focus Publications Ltd,
Geanies House, Fearn, Ross-shire,
IV20 1TW, Scotland, U.K.
www.christianfocus.com

Cover design by Daniel van Straaten

Printed and bound by
Bell & Bain, Glasgow

All rights reserved. No part of this publication may be reproduced, stored in a retrieval system, or transmitted, in any form, by any means, electronic, mechanical, photocopying, recording or otherwise without the prior permission of the publisher or a licence permitting restricted copying. In the U.K. such licences are issued by the Copyright Licensing Agency, 4 Battlebridge Lane, London SE1 2HX. www.cla.co.uk.

Contents

Preface 7

Background 9

1. Setting of Family Worship: The Godly Home 21
2. The Case for Family Worship 27
3. Elements of Family Worship 49
4. Practice of Family Worship 61
5. Barriers to Family Worship 67
6. Catechizing 73
7. Parental Hopes 87
8. Bibliography 91

Preface

The Family Worship Book was published as the fruit of my search for resources for leading my own family in its devotional life.[1] Over the years I have heard from people all across the ecclesiastical spectrum as to its helpfulness to them. Thankfully, awareness of the importance of daily family prayers seems to have grown since 1998, a recent evidence of which is Rod Dreher's advocacy of it from an Eastern Orthodox perspective in his *The Benedict Option*. What remains a relative novelty today was a key element in the program of spiritual nurture for earlier generations of Reformed Protestants. The consensus was remarkable and the advocacy fervent. The following work will cite the work of a number of classic authors of the Puritan and Reformed tradition. In my experience, voices from the past are a helpful corrective of the biases of the present. Wading deeply in the convictions and practices of previous generations assists one in transcending the blind spots of one's own generation. My hope is that

---
1. Terry Johnson, *The Family Worship Book* (Geanies House, Fearn, Ross-shire, Great Britain: Christian Focus Publications, 1998).

Understanding Family Worship

this supplement to *The Family Worship Book* will help strengthen, clarify and enrich the devotional life of those families that absorb its content. We will begin in Chapter 1 by looking at the setting of family worship, the godly home, which provides the vital context in which family worship occurs. Next we will examine the biblical and theological arguments for daily family worship in Chapter 2, drawing from the Old and New Testaments as well as the classic authors.

Once the case for family worship has been made, we then move on to develop the elements or practices of which family worship consists (Chapter 3). The how-do's are not ignored, but elaborated in Chapter 4. Many struggle with establishing the disciplined practice of family worship, so we seek to listen to the counsel of the classic authors in Chapter 5. Finally, we discuss catechizing in Chapter 6. Together, this monogram provides a feast of classic Reformed insight. Enjoy!

Background

The Reformation is sometimes treated as though it were merely a movement of theological reform, or at most one of ecclesiastical reform. However, the logic of Protestant theology flowed out of the church and into the streets, as it were, touching all aspects of life. This can be seen in particular in the case of marriage and family.

BACKGROUND[1]

The Reformers maintained that God was to be glorified in the home as well as the church. 'Nothing caught the new clergy up more personally in the Reformation's transition from theory to real life,' says Harvard historian Steven Ozment, 'than the institution of marriage.'[2] As was the case with the reform of worship and church government, reforms of family life were theologically driven. The issue

---

1. Much of the opening section is adapted from T. L. Johnson, *The Case for Traditional Protestantism* (Edinburgh: The Banner of Truth Trust, 2004), 144-149.

2. Steven Ozment, *Protestants: The Birth of a Revolution* (New York: Doubleday, 1992), 151.

raised by the Reformation was this: where is the ideal Christian life lived? According to the pre-Reformation church, it was lived in a monastery or convent. Truly serious Christians, those truly devoted to Christ, would commit themselves to the monastic ideals of separation and celibacy. Marriage was honored, but rated below the cloistered life of perpetual virginity. This preference for monastic celibacy arose in the context of a theological commitment to works-righteousness and an ascetic philosophy of spiritual assent. The result was the reduced status of marriage. Steven Ozment says of the medieval church that 'by so exalting celibacy and the cloister as the supreme forms of individual and communal self-realization it indirectly demeaned marriage and family as an imperfect, second-class estate' (my emphasis).[3] For example, Ignatius Loyola (1491-1556), founder of the Jesuits, urged Roman Catholics in the fourth rule of his Spiritual Exercises (1548) 'to praise highly the religious life, virginity, and continence; and also matrimony, but not as highly.'[4] Marriage was seen, says Ozment, as 'an institution best shunned by knowledgeable males.' As for females, 'unmarried virgins and continent widows were always spiritually superior to wives and mothers, and marriage was a debased state in comparison with the life of the cloister.'[5]

---

3. Steven Ozment, *When Fathers Ruled: Family Life in Reformation Europe* (Cambridge, MA: Harvard University Press, 1983), 12.

4. Ibid., 10.

5. Ibid., 9.

Background

At the same time that the Reformation affirmed justification by faith alone, in Christ alone through grace alone, it rejected the ascetic ideal and affirmed marriage. Ozment claims that for both the German and Swiss Reformers, 'clerical marriage was as prominent a tenant as justification by faith.'[6] The Reformer's rejection of the celibate ideal 'was as great a revolution in traditional church teaching and practice as their challenge of the church's dogmas on faith, works, and the sacraments.'[7] 'The Protestant Reformers were … the first to set the family unequivocally above the celibate ideal,' continues Ozment, 'and to praise the husband and the housewife over the monk and the nun in principle.'[7] Where is the ideal Christian life to be lived? In a family. As another leading scholar affirms, 'Marriage and family replaced celibacy as the divinely ordained setting for a Christian life and salvation.'[8]

The critical event in this new view of marriage took place in 1525 when Luther married Katherine von Bora. Katherine, along with nine other recent escapees from a neighboring convent, arrived in Wittenberg in the spring of 1523. Luther aided all nine in finding husbands or positions, save one, Katherine. An arranged marriage

---

6. Ozment, *Protestants,* 151.

7. Ibid., 153.

8. Thomas Max Safley, 'Family,' in Hans J. Hillerbrand (ed.), *The Oxford Encyclopedia of the Reformation,* Volumes 1-4 (New York: Oxford University Press, 1996), 2:93; see also liturgical scholar Horton Davies (1926-2005) who attributes the rise of family worship to 'the new significance given to the family by the Reformers' (*The Worship of the English Puritans* [1948; Morgan, PA: Soli Deo Gloria Publications, 1997], 278).

Understanding Family Worship

fell through and a second was refused by Katherine. In the end Luther decided to marry her himself. Ozment suggests she had her eye on Luther from the beginning.[9] 'For heaven's sake, not this one,' some of Luther's friends protested.[10] On the 27th of June, 1525 they were married. 'I have made angels laugh and the devils weep,' he wrote Spalatin.[11]

One year later Katherine gave birth to a son, Hans. Luther wrote to a friend, 'My Katherine is fulfilling Genesis 1:28.'[12] Over the next eight years five more children arrived, for a total of three boys and three girls. They enjoyed over twenty years of marriage. Luther's marriage and family became the ideal which many followed. Home, wife, and children came to be seen as positive benefits, not grace-inhibiting burdens.

The Reformers brought a number of new ideals to marriage and family, not the least of which was to ennoble the task of child rearing. Luther was a vigorous defender of marriage and parenting. According to Ozment, 'He exalted the family in all its dimensions and utterly without qualification.'[13] Against the medieval tendency to either denigrate women as temptresses (like Eve) or exalt them as virgins (like Mary), the Reformers praised their divine vocation as wives and mothers. 'There is

---

9. Ozment, *When Fathers Ruled*, 17.

10. Roland H. Bainton, *Here I Stand: A Life of Martin Luther* (1950; Nashville: Abingdon Press, 1978), 288.

11. Ibid., 289.

12. Ibid., 293.

13. Ozment, *Protestants*, 165.

no power on earth that is nobler or greater than that of parents,' said Luther.[14] The greatest service that one could perform for humanity was to rear godly children. 'When a father washes diapers or performs some other mean task for his child,' said Luther, 'God with all His angels and creatures is smiling.'[15]

The new Protestant family was seen as the foundation of society. Marriage, says Ozment, was viewed as 'the foundation and nucleus of society and the divine instrument for its stability and reform.' Management of the household was seen 'as the highest human art.'[16] Fathers were seen as priests, families as 'little churches,' the home as 'the cradle of civilization.' Child rearing was understood as more than nutrition and hygiene. The spiritual welfare of the children was at the center of the family's concerns. During the Middle Ages the monasteries were communities of prayer. Wherever the Reformation took root, the responsibility for daily prayer shifted to the Christian home. Family worship in the home became a hallmark of Protestantism for generations and right up until the recent past.

Family worship was universally insisted upon by previous generations of Reformed Protestants. Its roots may be traced back to Reformation Geneva and behind them to the church fathers.[17] John Calvin (1509-1564)

---

14. Ozment, *When Fathers Ruled*, 132.

15. Ibid., 8.

16. Ibid., 9.

17. Oliver Heywood and others see evidence for family worship in the writings of Basil (330-379), Chrysostom (349-407), Cyprian (200-258), Augustine (354-430), and others ('The Family Altar,' *The Whole Works of*

Understanding Family Worship

states the ideal in his commentary on 1 Corinthians published in 1546 (Latin) and 1547 (French). Commenting on 1 Corinthians 16:19 and 'the church in their house,' that is, the house of Aquila and Pricilla, he speaks of how 'wonderful' it is that the title 'church' should be applied to a single family, and indeed adds, 'It is fitting that all the families of believers should be organized in such a way as to be so many little churches.'[18] Calvin's Genevan Catechism of 1542-45 included five prayers for use at home at the beginning and end of each day and at mealtimes. The printer Jean Rivery in 1561 borrowed a number of these prayers to develop a family devotional liturgy, a 'family worship book' if you will, to be used morning and evening. Calvin's role in developing this is unclear, 'but he certainly approved of parents and family heads leading their households in worship,' says Calvin scholar Elsie Anne McKee.[19]

From this humble beginning, family worship developed into a normative practice among Protestants. The later Reformers and Puritans commonly referred to the family as a 'little church,' as in the cases of

---

the Rev. Oliver Heywood, Volumes I-V [1825; Morgan, PA: Soli Deo Gloria Publications, 1999], IV:332); Church historian Philip Schaff (1819-1893) cites Chrysostom's advocacy that every house should be a church (Philip Schaff, *History of the Christian Church* [1867, 1910; Grand Rapids: Wm B. Eerdmans Publishing Co., 1994 reproduction of fifth edition, revised], 3:545).

18. John Calvin, *The First Epistle of Paul the Apostle to the Corinthians,* translator John W. Fraser, Calvin's Commentaries (1546, 1547; Grand Rapids: Wm. B. Eerdmans Publishing Co., 1960), 356.

19. Elsie Anne McKee (ed.), *John Calvin: Writings on Pastoral Piety* (New York: Paulist Press, 2001), 210.

Background

William Perkins (1558-1602), known widely as the father of English Puritanism, and Thomas Cartwright (1535-1603), the father of English Presbyterianism.[20] Family worship achieved confessional status in the *Westminster Confession of Faith* (1647), which teaches that God is to be worshiped 'in private families daily'(XXI.6). It is noteworthy that the Confession was first published with an introduction addressed 'To the Christian Reader, Especially Heads of Families' (my emphasis), as well as Thomas Manton's (1620-1677) 'Epistle to the Reader,' similarly urging family religion. 'A family is the seminary of Church and State,' said Manton; 'and if children be not well principled there, all miscarrieth.'[21] Immediately upon adopting the Confession, the Scottish Presbyterians adopted a 'Directory for Family-Worship' as well, prefaced by an Act of the General Assembly that warned of excommunication of any head of household who neglected 'this necessary duty.'[22] Manton, citing Baxter, describes neglect of family worship as 'covenant-breaking with God, and betraying the souls of their children to the devil.'[23]

---

20. William Perkins, *Oeconomic, or Household Government:* A Short Survey of the Right Manner of Erecting and Ordering a Family, according to the Scriptures (1609; London: John Haviland, 1631), 670. This has been published in Volume 10 of his collected works by Reformation Heritage Books.

21. Thomas Manton, 'Mr. Thomas Manton's Epistle to the Reader,' *Westminster Confession of Faith* (Inverness: Free Presbyterian Publications, 1985).

22. *Westminster Confession of Faith,* 418; Heywood agrees that those who do not conduct family prayer are 'not fit to be communicants' ('Family Altar,' *Works,* IV:366).

23. Manton, 'Epistle,' 8.

Understanding Family Worship

Richard Baxter (1615-1691), writing in his Christian Directory, maintains that 'a Christian family is a church.'[24] William Gurnall (1617-1679), in his classic *The Christian in Complete Armour*, summarizes the historic Reformed understanding of the duties of 'family religion':

> The church began at first in a family, and was preserved by the godly care of parents in instructing their children and household in the truths of God, whereby the knowledge of God was transmitted from generation to generation, and though now the church is not confined to such strait limits, yet every private family is as a little nursery to the church.[25]

Matthew Henry (1662-1714), who in so many ways represents the apex of Reformed pastoral theology, devoted a sermon to the subject, entitled 'A Church in the House.' The family, he says, 'is the nursery in which the trees of righteousness are reared, and afterwards are planted in the courts of our God.' Heads of households, he urges, 'must be as prophets, priests, and kings in their own families; and as such they must keep up family doctrine, family worship and family discipline.'[26] 'What

---

24. Richard Baxter, 'A Christian Directory,' *The Practical Works of Richard Baxter*, Volumes I-IV (1654-5, 1673; Ligonier, PA: Soli Deo Gloria Publications, 19th century reprint, 1990), 1:418.

25. William Gurnall, *The Christian in Complete Armour*, (1662 and 1665; Edinburgh: The Banner of Truth Trust, 1964), I:164.

26. Matthew Henry, 'A Church in the House,' in *The Complete Works of Matthew Henry: Treatises, Sermons, and Tracts*, Volumes I-II (1855; Grand Rapids: Baker Book House, 1979), I:251, 252; Swinnock says of the head of household: 'He is a priest to pray for them, a prophet to instruct them,

the liturgy of the hours was for monks of the Middle Ages, the discipline of family prayer was for the Puritans,' says Hughes O. Old. He continues, 'The Puritans, whether on the Connecticut frontier or in the heart of London, whether they were Cambridge scholars or Shropshire cotters, gave great importance to maintaining a daily discipline of family prayer.'[27]

John Newton (1725-1807), author of the beloved hymn, 'Amazing Grace,' regarded family worship as 'a duty and a privilege' as well as a 'universal obligation.'[28] The early American Presbyterian, Samuel Davies (1723-1761), refers to the family as 'the nursery of the church and state.'[29] This too was typical of Reformed commentators up to the recent past. Southern

---

and a king to govern them according to God's word' ('The Christian Man's Calling,' *The Works of George Swinnock,* Vol. I [Edinburgh: The Banner of Truth Trust, 1992], I:380); also William Gouge, *Of Domestical Duties* (1622; Puritan Reprints: Pensacola, FL: 2006), 287, 392.

27. Hughes O. Old, 'Matthew Henry and the Puritan Discipline of Family Prayer,' in John Leith (ed.), *Calvin Studies,* VII, 'Papers Presented at a Colloquium on Calvin Studies,' Davidson College, Davidson College Presbyterian Church, Davidson, NC, Jan. 28-29, 1994, 69; Of late, Roman Catholics have begun emphasizing the importance of family prayers. In the book of *Catholic Household Blessings and Prayers,* Christian homes are referred to as 'little churches' in which 'prayer must happen… if the Sunday assembly is to become a community of prayer' (Washington, DC: United States Catholic Conference, 1988, 4). *The Journal of the Liturgical Conference, Liturgy,* devoted an issue to the subject of 'Little Churches: Ritual in the Home' (Vol. 21, Nov. 4, 2006).

28. John Newton, 'Family Worship,' *The Letters of John Newton* (London: The Banner of Truth Trust, 1965), 88.

29. Samuel Davies, 'The Necessity and Excellency of Family Religion,' *The Godly Family: A Series of Essays on the Duties of Parents and Children* (Pittsburgh: Soli Deo Gloria Publications, 1973), 1.

Presbyterian Benjamin M. Palmer (1818-1902) describes the family as 'the original society from which the state emerges, and the church, and every other association known amongst men.'[30] Currently in print is a veritable 'Who's Who' of historic Reformed authors who commend in the strongest terms the discipline of daily (typically twice daily!) family devotions. In addition to Perkins, Cartwright, Manton, Baxter, Gurnall, and Henry, we may cite from the sixteenth and seventeenth centuries: Arthur Hildersham (1563-1632), William Gouge (1575-1653),[31] George Hamond (1620-1705),[32] Thomas Lye (1621-1684),[33] Samuel Lee (1625-1691),[34] Oliver Heywood (1630-1702);[35] joining Davies and Newton from the eighteenth centuries: Thomas Doolittle (1630-1707),[36] Philip Doddridge (1702-1751),[37]

---

30. Benjamin M. Palmer, *The Family in its Civil and Churchly Aspects* (1876; Harrisonburg, VA: Sprinkle Publications, 1981), 9; he adds, 'In the Family are to be found both the State and the Church in embryo' (209).

31. Gouge, *Domestical Duties*.

32. George Hamond, *The Case for Family Worship* (1694; Orlando FL: Soli Deo Gloria Publications, 2005).

33. Thomas Lye, 'By What Scriptural Rules May Catechizing Be So Managed as That It May Become Most Universally Profitable,' in *Puritan Sermons, 1659-1689* (1844; Wheaton: Richard Owen Roberts, 1981), II:99ff.

34. Samuel Lee, 'What Means May Be Used Towards the Concession of Our Carnal Relations,' in *Puritan Sermons, 1659-1689*, (1844; Wheaton: Richard Owen Roberts, 1981), I:142ff.

35. Heywood, 'Family Altar,' *Works*, I:285-418.

36. Thomas Doolittle, 'How May the Duty of Daily Family Prayer Be Best Managed for the Spiritual Benefit of Every One in the Family,' in *Puritan Sermons, 1659-1689* (1844; Wheaton: Richard Owen Roberts, 1981), I:194ff.

37. Philip Doddridge, 'Religious Education,' in Kistler (ed.), *The Godly*

Background

George Whitefield (1714-1770), and Jonathan Edwards (1703-1758);[38] joining Palmer from the nineteenth century: J. W. Alexander (1804-1859)[39] and Robert Murray M'Cheyne (1813-1843).[40] Edwards considered 'family order' so important that he included this charge in his 'Farewell Sermon' to the Northampton, Massachusetts congregation that had just fired him:

> Every Christian family ought to be as it were a little church, consecrated to Christ, and wholly influenced and governed by his rules. And family education and order are some of the chief means of grace. If these fail, all other means are likely to prove ineffectual. If these are maintained, all the means of grace will be likely to prosper and be successful.[41]

J. I. Packer credits the English Puritans, the most consistent heirs of the Reformation, with virtually creating the family as we have come to know of it in the English speaking world, saying '… in the same sense in which,

---

Family: A Series of Essays on the Duties of Parents and Children (Pittsburgh, PA: Soli Deo Gloria Publications, 1993).

38. George Whitefield, 'The Great Duty of Family Religion,' in Kistler (ed.), *The Godly Family: A Series of Essays on the Duties of Parents and Children* (Pittsburgh, PA: Soli Deo Gloria Publications, 1993).

39. James W. Alexander, *Thoughts on Family Worship* (Morgan, PA: Soli Deo Gloria Publications), 1990.

40. Robert Murray M'Cheyne, 'Family Government,' *Additional Remains of the Rev. Robert Murray M'Cheyne* (Edinburgh: Johnstone and Hunter, 1984).

41. Jonathan Edwards, 'Memoirs of Jonathan Edwards,' in *The Works of Jonathan Edwards,* Vol. 1 (1834; Edinburgh: The Banner of Truth Trust, 1974), ccvi; also Heywood: 'Christian families are churches' ('Family Altar,' *Works,* IV:320); Gouge, *Domestic Duties,* 11.

under God, they were creators of the English Christian Sunday, so they were creators of the English Christian marriage, the English Christian family, and the English Christian home.'[42] The Puritans and their successors extended the seminal thoughts of the Reformers, developing the foundational ideals of the Christian home, beginning with marriage and encompassing the roles of husbands, wives, and children. They produced an entirely new body of literature detailing the importance of the home and the duties of parents and children.

Throughout the nineteenth and into the twentieth century, books of family prayers were published regularly and denominational periodicals regularly contributed devotional helps for families. Vigorous warnings were issued by the older authors against the negligent. 'If in your houses God hath not a church, the devil will have a chapel,' Doolittle warned. 'If your houses be not nurseries for heaven, they will be breeding places for hell.'[43] Virtually the whole weight of Protestant history testifies to the importance of family worship.

---

42. J. I. Packer, *A Quest for Godliness: The Puritan Vision of the Christian Life* (Wheaton, IL: Crossway Books, 1990), 260.

43. Doolittle, 'Family Prayer,' *Puritan Sermons,* 2:258.

1
Setting of Family Worship: The Godly Home

If family worship is to be beneficial, it must be conducted in the context of parental devotion to Christ. The religious integrity of parents is crucial. Parental baptismal vows typically begin with parents vowing to provide 'a godly example' for their children.[1] The covenant of God with His people includes the promise 'to be a God to you and to your offspring after you' (Gen 17:7), a promise repeated by the Apostle Peter at Pentecost (Acts 2:39). The context within which the promises of God for our children are fulfilled is that of the godly home. Deuteronomy 6:4-9 envisions a home in which the things of God dominate:

> Hear, O Israel: The Lord our God, the Lord is one. You shall love the Lord your God with all your

---

[1]. 'Do you now unreservedly dedicate your child to God, and promise, in humble reliance upon divine grace, that you will endeavor to set before (him/her) a godly example, that you will pray with and for (him/her), and you will teach (him/her) the doctrine of our holy religion, and that you will strive, by all the means of God's appointment, to bring (him/her) up in the nurture and admonition of the Lord? (Vow #3, *The Book of Church Order,* Presbyterian Church in America).

> heart and with all your soul and with all your might. And these words that I command you today shall be on your heart. You shall teach them diligently to your children, and shall talk of them when you sit in your house, and when you walk by the way, and when you lie down, and when you rise. You shall bind them as a sign on your hand, and they shall be as frontlets between your eyes. You shall write them on the doorposts of your house and on your gates (Deut 6:4-9, cf. 4:9, 10; 5:29; 11:19; 28:4).

Love for God is to fill the hearts of the parents (6:4), as are the commands of God (6:4-6). Talk of God is to be the overflow of the heart. 'These words' of God 'shall be on your heart.' Spiritual things are to be pursued not legalistically, or formally, but enthusiastically. 'He that loves God,' says Henry, 'loves his Bible.'[2] 'Religion' must not be a Sunday morning thing which bears no relation to the rest of the week. Rather, it is to be an all-day, everyday thing, 'when you lie down, and when you rise,' and every moment in between. Moses envisions that the things of God will be the stuff of informal conversation all throughout the day. Parents are regarded as capable of having these conversations and are to be inclined, even eager to do so. They are to manifest a pervasive love for God and His Word.[3]

The parental pattern of behavior is vital. Parental hypocrisy will be detected quickly. Parental inconsistency

---

[2]. Matthew Henry, *Exposition of the Old and New Testament* in Six Volumes (London: James Nisbet & Co., n/d), comments on Deuteronomy 6:6, 7.

[3]. Gouge, *Domestical Duties*, 395.

Setting of Family Worship: The Godly Home

will be exploited early. 'Your evil example,' says Hamond, will 'prejudice them more than your instructions and prayers will edify them.'[4] Henry entitles Psalm 101 'the house-holder's psalm,' noting the commitment which David, as head of his house, makes:

> I will walk with integrity of heart within my house;
>
> I will not set before my eyes anything that is worthless (Ps 101:2b-3a).[5]

The head of the house is responsible for both his own conduct, that it be exemplary, and that his household be kept free of evil: 'I will know nothing of evil' (Ps. 101:4).

George Swinnock in his classic 'The Christian Man's Calling,' says of a father's example that children will 'sooner follow their poisonous patterns than their pious precepts.'[6] Likewise Richard Baxter warns, 'They will sooner believe your bad lives than your good words.'[7] 'They are prone to imitate practices than to learn principles,' adds the Puritan Thomas Lye (1621-1684).[8] J. C. Ryle cites Archbishop Tillotson (1630-1694):

> To give children good instruction and a bad example, is but beckoning to them with the head to show them

---

4. Hamond, *Family Worship*, xviii.

5. Henry, *Exposition*, introductory comments on Psalm 101; see also Lee, 'Conversion,' *Puritan Sermons*, 1:146; Gouge, *Domestical Duties*, 395.

6. Swinnock, 'Christian Man's Calling,' *Works*, I: 416.

7. Baxter, 'Christian Directory,' *Works*, 1:453.

8. Lye, 'Profitable Catechizing,' *Puritan Sermons*, 2:125.

Understanding Family Worship

the way to heaven, while we take them by the hand and lead them in the way to hell.[9]

Parents teach by modeling holy living. As they exhibit sacrificial love, honesty, integrity, the fruit of the Spirit, and the Beatitudes, they teach. They are meant to be examples of Christ to their children, not perfectly, but truly. This is the environment in which the Christian message has integrity, in which the parental faith has credibility in the outlook of the children.

The parental pattern of commitment also is vital. The children will early perceive if parents are committed to love in the marriage, or merely tolerate each other. The children will soon know if their parents are committed to God with all their heart, soul, and mind, or if other gods are tolerated, indeed come first before God (Deut. 6:5). Children will quickly detect if their parents are committed to the church and its ministry, or if the church may safely be jettisoned if something perceived to be more valuable, more exciting, or more fun comes along. There is no replacing the parental role. Their example is vital.

What we say to our children is important. This is not being denied for a moment. However, our words must be built on the foundation of our deeds. What we profess must be matched by how we act. For a parent to say, 'Do as I say, not as I do,' is an exercise in futility. For a smoker to say, 'Don't smoke' or a drunkard to say, 'Don't

---

9. J. C. Ryle, *The Duties of Parents* (Sand Springs, OH: Grace and Truth Books, 2002; first published in *The Upper Room: Being Truth for the Times*. London: William Hunt & Co., 1888), 27.

drink' rarely works. For parents to drop their children for Sunday School and expect them to take 'religion' seriously is foolhardy. What is being modeled will defeat what is being urged. Children are sharp enough to see the reality or the lack thereof behind the words. What parents actually believe is true or important is evident in their actions, which as the saying goes, speak louder than words. A parental model of consistent godliness is the context in which family worship is designed to function. 'Do not forget,' Ryle warns us, 'that children learn more by the eye than they do by the ear. No school will make such deep marks on character as the home. Imitation is a far stronger principle than memory.'[10]

---

10. Ibid.

2
The Case for Family Worship

How are we to make the case for family worship? The classic authors help us. They recognize that there isn't a single passage or command that requires it. Instead, it is from the whole tenor of Scripture that the case is to be made. Hamond in particular rebuffs those who in connection with the duty of family worship demand 'the express words of Scripture' and like the Sadducees, in connection with the resurrection of the dead (Matt. 22:32-32), fail to draw proper deductions from Scripture, thereby missing what 'by sound and necessary consequences' can be know from Scripture.[1] The champions of family worship argue on the basis of the biblical examples of parental responsibility for the religious disposition of the family, as well as on the basis of right deductions rooted in the nature of things.

---

1. Hamond, *Family Worship*, 94, 93. His language echoes that of *Westminster Confession of Faith* 1.6.

Biblical Case: Old Testament

We may begin with the Old Testament examples of family religion. 'Religion was first hatched in families,' says Manton, 'and there the devil seeketh to crush it.' There was a time, he argues, when 'the families of the Patriarchs were all the Churches God had in the world.'[2] Abel offered a sacrifice that pleased God (Gen. 4:4). Where did he learn to do so? Such knowledge would have to have been passed on to him by his father Adam (cf. Gen. 3:21). True religion was passed from Adam to Seth to Enosh. From father to son the knowledge of what it meant to 'call upon the name of the Lord' was transmitted (Gen. 4:25, 26). We are told Enoch 'walked with God' (Gen. 5:24). Where did he learn to do so? From his father Jared. Enoch fathered Methuselah, Methuselah fathered Lamech, and Lamech fathered Noah, who also 'walked with God' (Gen. 6:9). From father to son, the knowledge of a godly walk was passed along.

Abraham was commended as one who 'command(ed) his children and his household after him to keep the way of the Lord by doing righteousness and justice,' a text featured prominently in the classic literature (Gen 18:19).[3] As head of the household, he commanded

---

2. Manton, 'Epistle,' 7.

3. E.g. Perkins, *Oeconomie,* 669, 698; Arthur Hildersham, 'Disciplining Children,' *The Godly Family: A Series of Essays on the Duties of Parents and Children* (Morgan, PA: Soli Deo Gloria Publications, 1993),108, 116, 132; Gouge, *Domestical Duties,* 392; Lee, 'Conversion,' *Puritan Sermons,* 1:152; Doolittle, 'Family Prayer,' *Puritan Sermons,* 226; Whitefield, 'Family Religion,'39, 42; Doddridge, 'Religious Education,'64; Davies,

his children to 'keep the way of the Lord.' Does this not assume that he knows 'the way of the Lord?' Would the 'way of the Lord' not include comprehensive instruction in the attributes, nature, commands, requirements, and worship of the Lord? He adds, 'by doing righteousness and justice.' Does this not require that Abraham teach his children what is meant by 'righteousness' and 'justice?' 'Abraham will not leave his children ... to their own genius, counsels, lusts, ignorance, idleness, superstitions, idolatry, but "command" them,' says Thomas Lye in his sermon on 'Profitable Catechizing.'[4] He must teach his children comprehensively the things of God. The responsibility is Abraham's. There is no school to which he may turn. There is no church to which he may delegate the responsibility. There is no Sunday School to which he may send his children.

Isaac and Jacob built altars wherever their families pitched their tents, the altar being 'a necessary utensil for divine worship' (Gen. 26:25; 28:18; 33:20; 35:1-3), says Davies.[5] The latter of these texts was the basis upon which Oliver Heywood (1624-1702) wrote his 133-page treatise, A Family Altar, (1693), where he demonstrates that Jacob, 'as a householder' (Gen. 35: 2, 3), by teaching his family its duty (v. 3), by building an altar and making an offering (v. 14), and by commanding his family to put away idols (v. 4), 'acts the part of a prophet, priest,

---

'Family Religion,'17.

4. Lye, 'Profitable Catechizing,' *Puritan Sermons,* 2:107.

5. Davies, 'Family Religion,'18.

Understanding Family Worship

and king.'[6] This Jacob did wherever he went, as did Abraham and Israel before him. This leads Heywood to the conclusion 'that governors of families must as priests erect family-altars for God's worship.'[7] Lye summarizes the pattern of religious instruction from Adam to Moses: 'how was the true religion communicated, but by oral tradition from parents to their children.'[8]

As we move from the Abrahamic to the Mosaic covenant, we read this exhortation from Moses to parents:

> And these words that I command you today shall be on your heart. You shall teach them diligently to your children, and shall talk of them when you sit in your house, and when you walk by the way, and when you lie down, and when you rise (Deut. 6:6, 7; 11:19, etc).

'Means are here prescribed for the maintaining and keeping up of religion in our hearts and houses,' says Henry.[9] Both the heart and the house are in view. 'Diligently' parents are to teach the children to love (Deut. 6:4) and obey God (6:7). They are constantly to teach them to do so. Hebrew expresses comprehensiveness through contrasts. When we 'sit' and when we 'walk,' when

---

6. Heywood, 'Family Altar' *Works,* IV:285-418.

7. Ibid., 297; see Doolittle, 'Family Prayer,' *Puritan Sermons,* 2:238.

8. Lye, 'Profitable Catechizing,' *Puritan Sermons,* 2:106.

9. Henry, *Exposition,* on Deuteronomy 6:6-7; also Perkins, *Oeconomie,* 670, 698; Hildersham, 'Disciplining Children,' 110, 113, 125; Gouge, *Domestical Duties,* 392, 395, 401; Doolittle, 'Family Prayer,' *Puritan Sermons,* 2:217; Lee, 'Conversion,' *Puritan Sermons,* 1:150, 151, 155; Doddridge, 'Religious Education,' 126; Davies, 'Family Religion,' 18.

The Case for Family Worship

we 'lie down' and when we 'rise' represent all of life and all the time. It means, says Matthew Poole (1624-1679), that this instruction is to be done 'diligently, earnestly, frequently, discreetly, and dexterously.'[10]

> You shall bind them as a sign on your hand, and they shall be as frontlets between your eyes. You shall write them on the doorposts of your house and on your gates (Deut. 6:8, 9).

Bibles were uncommon then. So they made do. They compensated by writing verses on their doorposts and gates, constantly reminding them of God's Word (cf. Exod. 13:9). The things of God are to be the theme of our households, constantly before our eyes, constantly in our conversations, going with us wherever we go. We who have completed Bibles in our hands may draw the necessary implications. The Scriptures are to be in the center of our homes, dominating family life.

This command to parents to teach their children is repeated three times in Deuteronomy, so important is their doing so for the future of the people of God (4:9, 10; 6:6, 7; 11:19; cf. 32:46).

Passover instruction was particularly the duty of families. 'When your children say to you, "What do you mean by this service?" you shall say, "It is the sacrifice of the Lord's Passover"' (Exod. 12:26, 27a). The children ask, the parents explain. Parents were to tell their sons and grandsons of the mighty signs wrought by God in

---

10. Matthew Poole, *A Commentary on the Whole Bible*, Volumes I-III (1683-85, 1865; Edinburgh: The Banner of Truth Trust, 1963), I:350.

Understanding Family Worship

the exodus (Exod. 10;1, 2). Parents were to teach their children the Ten Commandments (Deut. 4:9, 10ff). Parents were to teach their children of the parting of the waters of the Red Sea and then the Jordan River as the people of Israel passed into the Promised Land (Josh. 4:6, 7, 21, 22). If Old Testament parents were required to explain the work of redemption, the Ten Commandments, and the sacraments (circumcision and Passover) to their children, it is doubtful that Christian parents are expected to do any less. 'The good ruler of his family,' says Hamond, 'must then be a diligent and constant teacher of his household.'[11]

Joshua, though 'very much in public affairs,' though a very busy man leading a whole nation's military and religious affairs, yet neglects not his family,' Gouge points out. He thereby 'setteth himself first as a guide to the rest.'[12] Joshua modeled the priorities of godly men. He committed his family to God saying, 'As for me and my house, we will serve the Lord' (Josh. 24:15), the seminal text upon which Thomas Doolittle based his sermon, 'The Duty of Family Prayer,' and George Whitefield (1714-1770) his sermon, 'The Great Duty of Family Religion.'[13] Doolittle points out with multiple references

---

11. Heywood, 'Family Altar,' *Works,* IV:313; Davies, 'Family Religion,' 20, 21; Hamond, *Family Worship,* 29; cf. Doolittle, 'Family Prayer,' *Puritan Sermons,* 2:217.

12. Gouge, *Domestical Duties,* 395.

13. Whitefield, 'Family Religion,' 30-47; see also Perkins, *Oeconomie,* 669, 698; Hildersham, 'Disciplining Children,' 108, 111, 132; Lee, 'Conversion,' *Puritan Sermons,* 1:155; Philip Doddridge, 'A Plain and Serious Address on the Important Subject of Family Religion,' in *The Godly Family: A Series of Essays on the Duties of Parents and Children*

The Case for Family Worship

that the term 'to serve' is 'so comprehensive as to take in the whole worship of God' (e.g. Exod. 3:12; Deut. 6:12; 1 Sam. 7:3; Ps. 2:11; etc; and Matt. 4:10; Luke 1:74; Acts 7:7, etc.).[14] Whitefield argues from this text that 'every governor of a family ought to look upon himself as obliged to act in three capacities: as a prophet to instruct; as a priest to pray for and with; as a king to govern, direct and provide for them.' Further, 'every house is, as it were, a little parish... every family a flock.'[15] Davies builds his case on 1 Timothy 5:8.

> But if anyone does not provide for his relatives, and especially for members of his household, he has denied the faith and is worse than an unbeliever.

The provision for the family which the Apostle requires surely may not be restricted to that which is merely physical or material. If one who fails to provide physical necessities of life is worse than an unbeliever, 'What shall we say of him that restricts their souls?' he asks.[16]

We may point to the example of Job, of whom we read,

> And when the days of the feast had run their course, Job would send and consecrate them, and he would rise early in the morning and offer burnt offerings

---

(Morgan, PA: Soli Deo Gloria Publications, 1992]), 64; Davies, 'Family Religion,' 5; Heywood, 'Family Altar,' *Works,* IV:316; Gouge, *Domestical Duties,* 13, 395.

14. Doolittle, 'Family Prayer,' *Puritan Sermons,* 200. He also points out that the Hebrew word 'to save' in Joshua 24:15 (*abad*) is translated in the LXX by the word *latreuō,* 'to worship.'

15. Ibid., 32, 33; cf. Hamond, *Family Worship,* 103.

16. Davies, 'Family Religion,'5; also Perkins, *Oeconomie,* 670.

Understanding Family Worship

according to the number of them all. For Job said, 'It may be that my children have sinned, and cursed God in their hearts.' Thus Job did continually (Job 1:5).

Job 'would send' a message to them, to 'consecrate' themselves, a term used of preparing for the holy work of offering sacrifices (see Exod. 19:22; 1 Sam. 6:15; John 11:55).[17] 'We find Job so intent upon family devotion that he rises up early in the morning and offers burnt offerings' (Job 1:5), Davies notes.[18]

David, after restoring the ark to Jerusalem with a grand celebration, returned home to 'bless his family,' for what Davies calls 'his hour for family devotion' (2 Sam. 6:20).[19] Daniel 'went to his house' and 'got down on his knees three times a day and prayed and gave thanks before his God, as he had done previously' as was his custom (Dan. 6:10b). 'He had always observed a stated course of devotion in his family,' says Davies.[20]

Parents are urged in Proverbs, the Bible's ageless book of wisdom,

> Train up a child in the way he should go;
> even when he is old he will not depart from it
> (Prov. 22:6).

---

17. See Lye, 'Profitable Catechizing,' *Puritan Sermons,* 2:107.

18. Ibid., 18; see also Perkins, *Oeconomie,* 699; Hildersham, 'Disciplining Children,' 136; Gouge, *Domestical Duties,* 396; Lee, 'Conversion,' *Puritan Sermons,* 1:155, 166; Whitefield, 'Family Religion,' 34; Doddridge, 'Family Religion,' 64; Heywood, 'Family Altar,' *Works,* IV:317.

19. Ibid.; see also Doddridge, 'Family Religion,' 64; Heywood, 'Family Altar,' *Works,* IV:317.

20. Ibid.; see also Doolittle, 'Family Prayer,' *Works,* 2:230; Whitefield, 'Family Religion,' 35, 39.

The Case for Family Worship

'Train up,' 'or catechize,' says Thomas Lye; 'piously and prudently instruct and educate.'[21] Upon this text Lye based his sermon 'Profitable Catechizing.' The 'way' is literally 'the mouth of his way,' meaning early, from the beginning. A form of the word 'train' is used in Genesis 14:14 of Abram's 'trained' men, that is, men trained for warfare. The analogy of military training is useful. One trained for combat would have undergone extended instruction and repeated practice in the use of slings, shields, knives, spears, bows and arrows, as well as tactics and strategy. David says, 'Blessed be the Lord, my rock, who trains my hands for war, and my fingers for battle' (Ps. 144:1).

A child is to be trained in the way he should go, not the way he would go, but the way his parents would have him go. What is the 'way' that the child 'should go?' Would this not have to be explained? Would the child not have to be 'trained' in the way of truth? Would that not have to be contrasted with error? Would the child not have to be trained in the way of what is morally right, and would that not have to be contrasted with moral error? All this must be done early and constantly. This is what the Bible expects of parents while it promises that children will not 'easily and ordinarily' depart from that way, as Poole explains.[22]

Listen to the psalmist:

---

21. Ibid. See also Lee, 'Conversion,' *Puritan Sermons,* 1:151.
22. Poole, *Commentary,* II:257.

> He established a testimony in Jacob and appointed a law in Israel, which he commanded our fathers to teach to their children, that the next generation might know them, the children yet unborn, and arise and tell them to their children, so that they should set their hope in God and not forget the works of God, but keep his commandments (Ps. 78:5-7).

This is a remarkable statement describing how the faith is to be transmitted from one generation to the next. God 'commanded our fathers' to do what? 'To teach their children' (Ps. 78:5b). What are they to teach? God's law, His torah, His fatherly instruction. To what immediate end? So that those children, when they have their own families, might 'tell (the same) to their children,' and so on to one generation after another (Ps. 78:6). Teach to what ultimate end? 'So that they should set their hope in God' (Ps. 78:7a). The aim is that their children should know God to be One in whom they can hope, One who is good, and kind, and faithful, and just, and holy. Also, 'that they should ... not forget the works of God' (Ps.78:7b). They should know not only God's character and attributes, but His redemptive works, His 'glorious deeds and his might and the wonders he has done' (Ps. 78:4). For the psalmist, this meant the exodus, the primary redemptive event of the Old Testament, but for us it means, in addition, the ultimate redemptive event, the cross of Christ. They were also to be taught to 'keep his commandments' (Ps. 78:7b). The laws, the commands, and the will and Word of God were to be taught. Again, who is doing the teaching? Fathers. God 'established a testimony in Jacob and appointed a law in Israel,' and this law is what fathers are commanded to 'teach to their children' (Ps. 78:6; Ps. 34:11).[23]

An entire book of the Bible, Proverbs, presents itself as a father's instruction to his sons. Neither David nor Solomon appeared to be effective fathers, yet they knew better than they performed. Proverbs is a model of that which fathers are responsible to do for their children.[24] 'Hear, my son,' he says,

> your father's instruction, and forsake not your mother's teaching (Prov 1:8).

He says again,

> My son, if you receive my words and treasure up my commandments with you (Prov. 2:1).

And again,

> My son, do not forget my teaching, but let your heart keep my commandments, for length of days and years of life and peace they will add to you (Prov 3:1-2).

And again, and again, and again fathers are told to teach their children (Prov 3:21; 4:1, 10, 20; 5:1; 6:1, 20; 19:27; 23:15-26; 24:13, 21; 27:11) for a total of seventeen times in the first twenty-six chapters. What does the father teach his children? Everything. He begins with 'the fear

---

23. See Lee, 'Conversion,' *Puritan Sermons,* 1:146; Hilderbrand, 'Disciplining Children,' 110; Gouge, *Domestical Duties,* 392; Doddridge, 'Religious Education,' 187.

24. See Perkins, *Oeconomie,* 699; Lye, 'Profitable Catechizing,' *Puritan Sermons,* 2;107.

Understanding Family Worship

of the Lord' as the foundation of all true 'knowledge' (Prov. 1:7). For his son to fear the Lord would require knowing who the Lord is, what the Lord requires, and what fear is. He must pursue wisdom and 'the knowledge of God' because God is the source of 'knowledge and understanding' (Prov. 2:6).[25]

This godly father throughout Proverbs teaches his son of the importance of his words, of avoiding temptation, of the dangers of alcohol, of the dangers of pride, of care in choosing friends, of care in choosing a wife, of care in handling money, of diligence in work. He teaches him to fear God and obey God and trust God and serve God and commit himself to God. He teaches him of God's judgment, God's sovereignty, God's discipline, and above all, to pursue God's wisdom.

The Bible doesn't let mothers off the hook either. 'Forsake not your mother's teaching' (torah), sons are urged (Prov. 1:8; 6:20). King Lemuel, the source of the 31st chapter of Proverbs, records the wisdom 'that his mother taught him.' Lye understands King 'Lemuel' to mean 'of God,' meaning Solomon, who was chosen 'of God' to rule. His mother is Bathsheba.[26] 'What

---

25. See Lye, 'Profitable Catechizing,' *Puritan Sermons,* 2:107; Gouge, *Domestical Duties,* 397-99, 401.

26. Lye, 'Profitable Catechizing,' *Puritan Sermons,* 2:108. This identification of Solomon with King Lemuel, and Bathsheba with the instructing mother, was typical of the older authors. Poole claims 'the general consent of both Jewish and Christian authors.' Likewise the translation of Lemuel 'of or *from God* or belonging *to God*' was understood as a mother's term of endearment (Poole, *Commentary,* II:276; cf. John Trapp, *A Commentary on the Old and New Testaments,* Volumes I-V [1647, 1865-68; Eureka, CA: Tansky Publications, 1997], III: 149, 150; Henry

are you doing, my son?' she asks twice as she begins her exhortation (Prov. 31:1-2; cf. 1:8). So it was that Timothy was taught the Scriptures by his mother Eunice and grandmother Lois (2 Tim. 3:15-17; 2 Tim. 1:5). Devout parents provide their children with thorough instruction in the paths of godly wisdom. 'The good ruler of his family must be a diligent and constant teacher of his household,' says the Puritan George Hamond (1620-1705).[27]

Biblical Case: New Testament

As we examine the New Testament, we note that commonly the older writers refer to Jesus' band of disciples as His 'family' and note the regularity with which they prayed together (Luke 9:18; 11:1) and Jesus taught them privately (Mark 4:34; Matt. 15:15; Mark 13:3-4). This pattern He intended for us to see as an example, that we might pray with the members of our own family.[28]

The Apostle Paul refers three times to churches that meet in private houses (Rom. 15:5; 1 Cor. 16:19; Col. 4:15; Philemon 2; see also Acts 4:23-31 and Acts 12), the second of these providing the text upon which Henry based his sermon. B. M. Palmer (1818-1902) cites these texts as 'giving evidence that the earliest Christian

---

Exposition, on Proverbs 31:1ff; Lee, 'Conversion,' *Puritan Sermons,* 1:152, 166; Gouge, *Domestical Duties,* 395, 398; more modern authors such as Charles Bridges' *Commentary on Proverbs,* disagree [1847; Edinburgh: The Banner of Truth Trust, 1968], 616).

27. Hamond, *Family Worship,* 29.

28. Perkins, *Oeconomie,* 699; Hamond, *Family Worship,* 72-76.

organizations were formed within the enclosure of the family.'[29] The centurion Cornelius is called 'a devout man who feared God with all his household' who 'prayed continually' (Acts 10:2, 30). Hamond identifies this as a 'plain and pregnant ... proof that Cornelius maintained family worship.' To fear God 'with all house' (*oikos*) 'at least necessarily includes his worshiping God in and with his family.'[30] Immediately following the Apostle's directions regarding various domestic relations in Colossians 3:18–4:1 (wives, husbands, children, fathers, etc.), he then exhorts,

> Continue steadfastly in prayer, being watchful in it with thanksgiving (Col 4:2).

Is he not still addressing families? Families, as families, are to 'continue steadfastly in prayer.'

Similarly, the Apostle Peter provides directions for wives and husbands, concluding with the warning to the latter to live with the former in an 'understanding way ... so that your prayers may not be hindered' (1 Pet. 3:1-7). 'Family-disorders hinder family prayer,' Doolittle warns. Whose prayers? The prayers of husband and wife together, which prayers the Apostle assumes are a characteristic family practice.[31]

---

29. Palmer, *The Family,* 207; see also Perkins, *Oeconomie,* 670; Davies, 'Family Religion,' 19; Heywood, 'Family Altar,' *Works,* IV:321.

30. Hamond, *Family Worship,* 77; see also Perkins, *Oeconomie,* 669; Hildersham, 'Disciplining Children,' 108; Lee, 'Conversion,' *Puritan Sermons,* 1:157; Whitefield, 'Family Religion,' 34; Davies, 'Family Religion,' 19; Heywood, 'Family Altar,' *Works,* IV:317.

31. Doolittle, 'Family Prayer,' *Puritan Sermons,* 2:238; cf 229, 250.

The Case for Family Worship

General duties that are common to Christians may be applied to families. Are Christians not to exhort and instruct one another (Heb. 3:13; Rom. 15:14)? Are they not to teach and admonish one another (Col. 3:16)? 'How much more, then,' Davies asks, 'is it our duty to teach, admonish and exhort our families, which are more particularly entrusted to our care?'[32] Are Christians not to pray for each other (James 5:16)? Are they not to sing praises with each other (Col. 3:16; Eph. 5:19)? Are they not to give thanks in everything (1 Thess. 5:17, 18; Phil. 4:6; Col. 4:2)? 'Oh, sirs,' Davies exclaims, 'the case is so plain, you need no time to deliberate.'[33] Of course families should pray and sing praises together. It is obvious. 'What intelligent Christian can disagree?' Doddridge asks.[34] Davies warns, 'If you are determined to resist convictions and live in willful neglect of this duty … your families are like to be nurseries for hell,' and, he says, 'I must discharge the artillery of heaven against you.'[35] Finally we turn to the Apostle's admonition to parents:

> Fathers, do not provoke your children to anger, but bring them up in the discipline and instruction of the Lord (Eph. 6:4).

---

32. Davies, 'Family Religion,' 21.

33. Ibid. See also Heywood, 'Family Altar,' *Works,* IV:322; Doolittle, 'Family Prayer,' *Puritan Sermons,* 2:229-230.

34. Doddridge, 'Family Religion,' 51.

35. Ibid., 22, 23.

Understanding Family Worship

The Apostle Paul uses this term, 'instruction' (*narthesia*) elsewhere, in connection with lessons from the Old Testament. 'They were written down for our instruction,' he says (1 Cor. 10:11). Charles Hodge (1797-1878) is happy with the old translation, 'admonition,' and defines it as 'the act of reminding one of his faults or duties.' They are to be thoroughly instructed, he continues, 'so that they be brought to knowledge, self-control, and obedience.'[36] Parents, fathers in particular, are to teach their children the things of God. Our children are to be 'instructed in the Lord,' meaning provided with instruction 'drawn and fetched from the word of the Lord,' says Lye.[37] They must be nurtured, he continues,

> not only in arts and sciences, to make them worldly wise and learned; nor only in the mysteries of trading and worldly employment, to make them rich; nor only in matters of morality and civil honesty, to make them sober and virtuous; but in the mysteries of true religion.[38]

We may conclude that divine method of transmitting the faith from one generation to the next is by family-based instruction. 'Our great care,' says Henry, 'must be to lodge our religion, the great deposit, pure and entire in the hands of those who succeed us.'[39] The family is at

---

36. Hodge, *Ephesians*, 264; see also Hildersham, 'Disciplining Children,' 110, 119; Lee, 'Conversion,' *Puritan Sermons*, 1:151; Doolittle, 'Family Prayer,' *Puritan Sermons*, 2:217; Whitefield, 'Family Religion,' 39.

37. Lye, 'Profitable Catechizing,' *Puritan Sermons*, 2:106.

38. Ibid., 2:106.

39. Henry, *Exposition*, on Psalm 78:4.

the center of God's kingdom program, Old Testament and New Testament, from Abraham to Moses to David, to the Apostle Paul, to today.

CASE FROM NATURAL REVELATION AND REASON

Not only may we agree on the basis of Scripture, but also on the basis of natural revelation or what we might call sanctified common sense. Families, as families, receive the blessings of God, sin against God, and depend on God. Are families not obligated as families to thank God, confess their sins to God, and seek His help and care? Heywood makes the case forcefully:

> There are daily cases, occasions, and necessities that require families, to be presented to the Lord. There are family sins to be confessed, wants to be enumerated, mercies to be desired, cares and crosses to be removed, fears to be prevented, temptations to be resisted, duties to be performed, graces to be exercised, peace to be maintained or regained, passions to be suppressed, mercies to be acknowledged; and all these must be laid at God's feet in daily prayer. That is a rare family which hath not some prodigal son, or carnal soul, as a member of it; some body sick in it, or some child to dispose of in marriage, or to employ in some occupation; some doubts or difficulties that call for prayer, wherein the whole family is concerned; or if there be no such exigency at present, yet who knows how soon any of these, or all these may light upon a family? and what remedy is there like family prayer?[40]

---
40. Heywood, 'Family Altar,' *Works,* IV:222-223; cf. Doolittle, 'Family

Understanding Family Worship

Whitefield speaks of

> the reasonableness of family religion.' He asks, 'Must not your conscience presently tell you it is fit that persons who receive so many mercies together should acknowledge them together?'[41]

Since without God's support and blessing our families would 'sink into ruin,' are we not, then, 'obliged in a family capacity to acknowledge and praise Him?' Davies asks.[42] At the beginning of the day,

> Dare you venture your families out into the world all the day without committing them to the care of Providence in the morning?[43]

At the end of the day,

> How can you venture to sleep without committing yourself and yours to the divine protection, and returning thanks for the mercies of the day?[44]

Similarly, Whitefield points out that

> there are no families but what have some common blessings of which they have been all partakers to give thanks for; some common crosses and afflictions which they are to pray against; some common sins which they are all to lament and bewail.

Prayer,' *Puritan Sermons,* 2:212-216; 235-236.
41. Whitefield, 'Family Religion,' 52.
42. Davies, 'Family Religion,' 11.
43. Ibid., 24.
44. Ibid.

The Case for Family Worship

So he asks, 'But how this can be done without joining together in one common act of humiliation, supplication, and thanksgiving is difficult to devise.' 'Family prayer,' he says, 'is a great and necessary duty.'[45]

The classic writers also utilize practical arguments. Family worship, Whitefield argues, is also the 'most proper' and effective way of teaching one's children the Christian faith. He cites the example of the family's prayers:

> They may learn to conceive aright of the divine perfections when they hear you daily acknowledging and adoring them. Their hearts may be touched early with remorse for sin when they hear your confessions poured out before God. They will know what mercies they are to ask for themselves by observing what turn your petitions take. Your intercessions may diffuse into their minds a spirit of love to mankind, a concern for the interest of the church and of their country… Your solemn thanksgivings for the bounties of Providence, and for the benefits of a spiritual nature, may affect their hearts with those impressions towards the gracious Author of all, which may excite in their little breasts love to Him, the most noble and genuine principle of all true and acceptable religion. Thus they may become Christians by insensible degrees, and grow in the knowledge and love of truth as they do in stature.[46]

He speaks of known examples of people who dated their conversions 'from the serious and pathetic prayers which

---

45 Whitefield, 'Family Religion,' 38.
46. Ibid., 58, 59; see also Alexander, *Family Worship,* 58-70; 82-93.

Understanding Family Worship

they have heard their pious fathers (and) pious mothers presenting before God on their account.'[47] Families committed to the duty of family worship become 'nurseries of piety,' he insists.[48] He terms it 'the greatest cruelty to your children to neglect' the eternal benefits that come from regular family worship.[49]

Baxter cites the many advantages of family discipline, teaching, and worship, even over the ministry of the church's pastors:

> 1. You have but a few to teach and rule, and the pastor hath many. 2. They are always with you, and you may speak to them as seasonably and as often as you will, either together, or one by one, and so cannot he. 3. They are tied to you by relation, affection, and covenant, and by their own necessities and interest otherwise than they are to him. Wife and children are more confident of your love to them than of the minister's; and love doth open the ear to counsel. Children dare not reject your words, because you can correct them, or make their worldly state less comfortable. But the minister doth all by bare exhortation; and if he cast them out of the church for their impenitence, they lose nothing by it in the world; and unless it be in a very hot persecution, families are not so restrained from holy doctrine, worship, and discipline, as churches and ministers often are. Who silenceth you and forbiddeth you to catechize and teach your family? Who forbiddeth you to pray or praise God with them, as well and as often as you can? It is self-condemning

---

47. Ibid., 58.
48. Ibid.
49. Ibid., 59.

The Case for Family Worship

hypocrisy in many rulers of families, who now cry out against them as cruel persecutors, who forbid us ministers to preach the gospel, while they neglect to teach their own children and servants, when no man forbiddeth them; so hard is it to see our own sins and duty, in comparison of other men's.

You have greater and nearer obligations to your family than pastors have to all the people. Your wife is as your own flesh; your children are, as it were, parts of yourself. Nature bindeth you to the dearest affection, and therefore to the greatest duty to them. Who should more care for your children's souls than their own parents? If you will not provide for them, but famish them, who will feed them? Therefore, as ever you have the bowels of parents, as ever you care what becometh of your children's souls for ever, devote them to God, teach them his word, educate them in holiness, restrain them from sin, and prepare them for salvation.[50]

Henry pleads with us,

I beg of you for God's sake, –for Christ's sake –for your own precious soul's sake, –and for your children's sake of your own bodies, that you will live no longer in the neglect of so great, and necessary, and comfortable a duty as this of family-worship is.[51]

---

50. Richard Baxter, 'Poor Man's Family Book,' *The Practical Works of Richard Baxter,* Volumes 1-4 (1654-5, 1673; Ligonier, PA: Soli Deo Gloria Publications, 1990), 4:231; see also Hildersham, 'Disciplining Children,'110-111; Gouse, *Domestical Duties,* 392-393; Lye, 'Profitable Catechizing,' *Puritan Sermons,* 2:110-112; Doddridge, 'Religious Education,' 194; Palmer, *The Family,* 282-290.

51. Henry, 'Church in the House,' *Works,* 1:264.

3
Elements of Family Worship[1]

What are the activities of family worship? What is the family actually to do during its devotions? There are three basic elements. 'As to the parts of family religion,' says Davies, 'they are prayer, praise, and instruction.'[2] Similarly, Doddridge urges us to honor God in our families 'by calling them together every day to hear some part of His Word read to them, and to join, for a few minutes at least, in your confessions, prayers, and praises to Him.'[3]

Prayer[4]

J. W. Alexander (1804-1859) identifies prayer as 'the essential part of Family Worship' and assigns to it 'the

---

1. See *Family Worship Book,* 18-21, 23-44.

2. Davies, 'Family Religion,' 8. The 'Directory for Family Worship' lists 'prayer and praises' and 'reading of the scriptures, with catechising in a plain way' (*Westminster Confession of Faith*, 419).

3. Doddridge, 'Family Religion,' 51; so also Baxter, 'Directory,' *Works,* 1:467; Newton, 'Family Worship,' *Letters,* 90; Alexander, *Family Worship*, 193ff; Hildersham, 'Disciplining Children,' 124.

4. See *Family Worship Book,* 26-31, 36-43, 98-107.

Understanding Family Worship

first place.'[5] According to Swinnock, 'Our houses are God's houses, and in God's house there must every day be morning and evening sacrifice.'[6] He continues:

> Families need direction in the day and protection in the night, and truly either of them is worth a prayer. Thy family sins must be pondered, thy family work must be supplied, and if they do not deserve a prayer they deserve nothing.[7]

Baxter argues that the family, as a family, both has needs and receives blessings from God. Consequently, 'It is the will of God that the family pray for these things when they need them, and give thanks for them when they have received them.'[8] Family prayers focus mainly on family concerns, many of which would be out of place in the public assembly. Baxter explains: 'Families have family necessities, which are larger than to be confined to a closet, and yet more private than to be brought still into the assemblies of the church.'[9] Yet 'there is no domestic want, danger, sorrow, or dispensation,' says Alexander of family prayers, 'which may not be remembered.'[10] Henry identifies five themes for the family's prayers: dependence upon God, confession of sin, thanksgiving for blessings,

---

5. Alexander, *Family Worship*, 195.

6. Swinnock, 'Christian Man's Calling,' *Works*, I:338. So also Baxter: 'family sins are daily committed, and family mercies daily received, and family necessities daily do occur' ('Directory,' *Works*, 1:421).

7. Ibid.

8. Baxter, 'Directory,' *Works*, 1:416.

9. Ibid., 1:419.

10. Alexander, *Family Worship*, 196.

Elements of Family Worship

petitions for mercy and grace, and intercessions for others.[11] 'In a word,' he concludes,

> let us go by this rule in our family devotions, –whatever is the matter of our care, let it be the matter of our prayer; and let us allow no care, which we cannot in faith spread before God: and whatever is the matter of our rejoicing, let it be the matter of our thanksgiving; and let us withhold our hearts from all those joys which do not dispose us for the duty of praise.[12]

Alexander urges brevity in family worship, especially in relation to prayer. 'Few things are more hardening and deadening in their influence,' he warns, 'than the daily recurrence of long and unwakening prayers.'[13] Prayers should be brief and varied, avoiding 'formalism and tediousness,' 'sameness and routine,' 'ritual coldness and emptiness.'[14]

For those sensing their inadequacy for leading their families in prayer, Heywood offers ten practical helps to assist those who when once upon their knees don't know what to say. We may highlight his recommendations under six categories.

1. **Attend a church with a powerful preaching ministry.** Solid, biblical preaching will facilitate solid, biblical praying. Under a faithful preaching ministry, Heywood maintains, 'You will hear directions, motives,

---

11. Henry, 'Church in the House,' *Works,* I:254-256.
12. Ibid., I:256.
13. Alexander, *Family Worship,* 197.
14. Ibid., 197-199.

precepts, promises, Scripture arguments to quicken and direct you in this practice; there you may gain knowledge of God the object of worship, of Christ the mediator and advocate, of the Holy Ghost that must assist you; there you will get a good understanding of God's mind and will, which will furnish you with ability, and further your acquaintance with God.'[15] Then pray, he says that 'the fruit of preaching will appear in your prayers as well as practice.'[16]

2. **Learn the Scriptures.** The Bible is the believer's prayer book. We must go to the Bible to learn how to pray. Like the disciples, we must say, 'Lord, teach us to pray' (Luke 11:1). The Scriptures provide us with the language with which to praise God, confess sin, give thanks, and offer our petitions. Sounding a common theme among Reformed Protestants, Heywood exhorts,

> If you be mighty in the Scriptures, you will be mighty in prayer. God loves to be spoken to in his own language; study Scripture precepts, and turn them into prayer, study Scripture promises, and turn them into pleas, study Scripture threatenings, and turn them into deprecations, and study Scripture patterns for imitation.[17]

There also are models of prayer from which we can learn: Abraham (Gen. 18:23-33); Jacob (Gen. 32:9, 12); Moses (Exod. 32:11-13); Joshua (Josh. 7:6-9); Hannah

---

15. Heywood, 'Family Altar,' *Works,* IV:378.
16. Ibid., 379.
17. Ibid., 379-380.

(1 Sam. 1:11); Solomon (1 Kings 3:6-9; 8:22-53); David (1 Chron. 17:16-27); Nehemiah (Neh.1:4-11); Ezra (Ezra 9); Daniel (Dan. 9); plus those of the Apostle Paul (Eph. 1, Phil. 1, Col. 1).[18] When reading the Bible, Heywood counsels, 'Think, now God is speaking to me, and thereby furnishing me with matter to speak to him in prayer.'[19]

3. **Pray an expanded Lord's Prayer. Elaborate upon each clause.** Don't repeat it formally or superstitiously, as though it were a charm. Don't 'rattle it over as a parrot,' Heywood warns.[20] He provides a model of what he means:

> *Our Father who art in heaven*: You are the common Father of all mankind, and our Father in Christ, we humbly and reverently prostrate ourselves at your footstool, in confidence of being received through Your well-beloved Son and our advocate: give us child-like affection for You, with endeared love to all Your people, and tender compassion for all others!
>
> *Hallowed be thy name*: let Your glorious titles, attributes, word and ordinances be manifested through the world, dispose all things to the glory of Your name, assist us in our confessing and forsaking our sins, adoring Your infinite perfections, believing in You, subjecting ourselves to You, attending on You, and aiming at Your glory in all we are, or do, or suffer.

---

18. Ibid., 380.
19. Ibid.
20. Ibid., 381.

Thy kingdom come: destroy, O Lord, the devil's kingdom of ignorance and wickedness, advance Your kingdom in converting sinners, building up Your church, maintaining the power of godliness, and hastening the kingdom of glory, confirming and preparing our souls for our Lord's second coming.

Thy will be done on earth as it is in heaven: let Your perceptive will be our rule, enable us to comply with it, give us knowledge of it, conquer the enmity of our stubborn wills, enable us to do Your will singly, sincerely, universally, and constantly, as angels and glorified saints; help us quietly to acquiesce in Your providential will, be it apparently for us or against us.

Give us this day our daily bread: vouchsafe to us a competent portion of outward comforts, for our daily supply, and Your blessing therewith, which is the staff of our bread, for we depend on You for all.

Forgive us our debts as we forgive our debtors: for Christ's sake and satisfaction, pardon all our sins; whereby we are indebted to divine justice, which we can never satisfy, but we lay hold by faith on the Lord our righteousness, and freely forgive all men their offences against us, and pray God to forgive them.

And lead us not into temptation, but deliver us from evil: Lord, we have depraved hearts, prevent occasions of sin, restrain the tempter, keep us out of harm's way, and make us conquerors of the world, the flesh, and the devil; let not sin have dominion over us.

For thine is the kingdom, the power, and the glory, for ever, Amen: we take not our encouragement in our prayers from any thing in ourselves, but from You who are the only sovereign, all-sufficient God, able and willing to help Your poor creatures; to You only be ascribed all dominion, blessing, honour, glory, and power, for evermore, amen, so be it.[21]

4. **Pray with God alone.** We cannot expect to pray well in public if we fail to pray well in private. 'First pray in your closets, and then you will be better able to pray in your families.'[22] In your prayer closet, 'you will find that God will suggest words to your minds, which you may employ in your families in prayer.'[23] Skill in public prayer is 'obtained by frequent conversing with God as our friend.'[24] He promises 'you will never want matter, or words, or enlargedness, if you be thus acquainted with God.' Indeed, 'your family will soon perceive that you have been with Jesus in secret, when they discern such freedom of speech and spirit.'[25]

5. **Pray with practical awareness.** Know your sins, needs, mercies, and dangers. Know what the Bible says about the nature of sin. This, Heywood says, 'will help you in confession, self-accusation, and deep humiliation, which is a considerable part of prayer.'[26] Citing the grief

---

21. Ibid., 382-383 (lightly modernized).
22. Ibid., 384.
23. Ibid.
24. Ibid., 385.
25. Ibid.
26. Ibid., 386.

expressed in 2 Chronicles 6:29 and the groaning of Psalm 38:9, he urges,

> Sorrow makes eloquent,... and if there be inward sighs, there will be outward speeches; if you be full of griefs, you will be full of complaints; if you be full of matter, you will speak that you may be refreshed (Job 32:18-20). Consult the book of conscience, and you will find it easy to draw up a large bill of indictment against your own souls.[27]

He explains further:

Know your needs. Know what you and your family lack. Know your weaknesses. 'Need makes beggars,' he says, 'and adds earnestness to prayers.'[28] Is a family member unconverted? Is another wavering? Is there a temptation or trial approaching? Is there sickness? Is there a challenge financially? Know your needs and you will plead with earnestness and eloquence.

Catalog your mercies. Recall the kindness of God that you have experienced personally, or as a family, both in temporal and eternal realms, both in material and spiritual things. Given that 'they are more than can be told' (Ps. 40:5), God's mercies provide us with abundant matter for praise and thanksgiving.

Know the dangers that threaten you. Heywood cites the Latin proverb, 'He that knows not how to pray, let him go to sea.' There are dangers on the roadways, dangers in air travel, dangers on the sea, dangers from fires, dangers

---

27. Ibid.
28. Ibid.

in the workplace, dangers from storms, dangers from thieves. 'Put yourselves into God's hands every morning and evening, for you are never safe but under his tuition, the omniscient, omnipotent God only can guard you and your family.'[29]

6. **Seek the help of the Holy Spirit**. Ask the Spirit to enable you to lead the family in its worship and especially to lead in prayer. Jesus promised to give the Holy Spirit to those who seek help in prayer (Luke 11:1, 13). The Apostle Paul identifies the role of the Holy Spirit in assisting us with our prayers.

> Likewise the Spirit helps us in our weakness. For we do not know what to pray for as we ought, but the Spirit himself intercedes for us with groanings too deep for words (Rom. 8:26).

Note that the Apostle says not that we don't know how to pray but for what to pray. 'We may be at a loss in particulars,' Heywood acknowledges, 'except the Spirit bring things into our thoughts, and often suggest Scripture expressions to our memories.'[30] He explains that the Spirit intercedes by helping His people to intercede. 'He prays,' says Heywood, 'by helping us to pray.'[31] The Puritan and Reformed tradition regards with the utmost seriousness the development of the gift of free prayer. Heywood insists that

---

29. Ibid., 388.
30. Ibid., 390.
31. Ibid.

They that have any solid experience in the things God, know that the assistance of the Spirit in prayer is the greatest reality in the world; nor was it a temporary gift, but a permanent grace abiding with the church for ever, enabling even private Christians to pray in the Spirit.[32]

READING SCRIPTURE[33]

Not only are prayers to be offered, but the Word is to be read. 'As by prayer thy duty is to acquaint God with thy family wants,' says Swinnock, 'so by reading some portion of Scripture daily, thy duty is to acquaint thy family with God's will.'[34] Typically the older authors recommend a chapter from the New Testament in the morning and a chapter from the Old Testament in the evening. Reading the books of the Bible in order is also recommended, though not exclusively, so as to rule out some discretion. There are times when the diet should be varied: historical narrative, poetry, wisdom, prophets, epistles, gospels, and so on. According to his biographer, Philip Henry (1631-1696), father of Matthew, while recognizing that 'one star in the firmament of Scripture differs from another in glory,' yet, 'whenever God hath a mouth to speak, we should have an ear to hear.'[35]

Although the head of house should not be expected to provide an exposition, 'It is certainly desirable,' says

---

32. Ibid., 391.

33. See *Family Worship Book,* 49-60, for an approach to family readings and record-keeping.

34. Swinnock, 'Christian Man's Calling,' *Works,* I:340; see Gouge, *Domestical Duties,* 286-287, 394; Henry, *Works,* 1:254.

35. J. B. Williams, *The Lives of Philip and Matthew Henry,* 2 Volumes in one (1698, 1828; Edinburgh: The Banner of Truth Trust, 1974), I:75.

Elements of Family Worship

Alexander, 'that a passing remark should now and then be thrown in, to explain a hard word, present a misconception, to apply a divine sentence to the heart.'[36] Care should be taken as to the manner of reading the Bible. Alexander is concerned that 'half its meaning, and almost all of its effect, are sometimes suffocated and lost, by a sleepy, monotonous, stupid, careless, inarticulate, drawling, or what is worse, an affected delivery.'[37] He urges that the best reader in the house should do the reading, 'with all solemnity and expression,' as 'the Scriptures cannot be read too well.'[38] Thus the master of the house fulfills two of his offices:

> O expecteth that thou shouldst be both a priest to offer up sacrifice for, and a prophet to instruct and teach thy family.[39]

Baxter counsels that a chapter be read, plus a few pages from a good book. So it is that 'holy families are the seminaries of Christ on earth.'[40]

SINGING OF PRAISES[41]

'I must not omit to recommend to you the singing of psalms in your families, as a part of daily worship,'

---

36. Alexander, *Family Worship,* 209.
37. Ibid., 212.
38. Ibid., 212, 213.
39. Ibid.; see Henry, 'Church in the House,' *Works,* I:254.
40. Baxter, 'Poor Man's Family Book,' *Works,* 4:237, 230; see also Newton, 'Family Worship,' *Letters,* 90.
41. See *Family Worship Book,* 119-197, for a recommended core of sixty hymns and sixty metrical psalms to learn, along with a ten-year schedule for doing so.

says Henry.[42] Not only does psalm-singing combine the elements of word and prayer (see Col. 3:16 and Eph. 5:19), but it also is especially appreciated by the children. Singing, he says, 'will warm and quicken you, refresh and comfort you.'[43] Henry published in 1694 *Family Hymns Gathered Mostly out of the Translations of David's Psalms for the use of families in their daily devotions.*[44]

Alexander complains that singing had ceased to be a part of family worship in many households in his day (writing in 1847). 'Domestic psalmody is productive of devotion,' he insists. Indeed, 'the singing of God's praise is eminently conducive to the awakening and maintenance of holy affections.'[45] It also helps prepare children for participation in public worship. Care should be taken that songs be sung from the heart, with understanding and with reverence (1 Cor. 14:15).

Prayer, the reading of Scripture, and the singing of praises are the three activities or elements of family worship. The family's devotional exercises are essentially simple. They can be conducted most anywhere, anytime, by any family. Beginners need not be intimidated, novices need not be cowed.

---

42. Henry, 'Church in the House,' *Works,* I:257.

43. Ibid.

44. Found in *Works,* I:413-443; see also Newton, 'Family Worship,' *Letters,* 90.

45. Alexander, *Family Worship,* 212.

4
Practice of Family Worship[1]

As we have seen above, all of the classic authors are concerned that family worship not be conducted with what Heywood calls 'mere customary formality.'[2] Those who call upon God must purge their hearts from sin (Ps. 66:18), rouse their sleepy souls to take hold of God (Isa. 64:7), and cultivate the proper motive of God's glory rather than mere duty or impressing others (Matt. 6:5-6). Pray for the assistance of the Holy Spirit.

> Let my prayer be counted as incense before you, and the lifting up of my hands as the evening sacrifice! (Ps. 141:2).

See to it that 'your heads and hearts be well furnished,' Heywood urges; 'your head with sound knowledge, and your hearts with saving grace.' Without these one will not be equipped to lead family worship. 'With the former you will have no ability, without the latter, you will have

---
1. See *Family Worship Book*, 17-18.
2. Heywood, 'Family Altar,' *Works,* IV:368.

no disposition for the practice,' he warns.[3] Among the necessary ingredients in leading family worship effectively are 'a submissive will, a renewed conscience,' and 'sanctified affections.'[4] Without these, Heywood continues, 'Your labor will be but lip-labor, and so lost labor; and all your piety will be but hypocrisy.'[5] 'Come to prayer with a lively heart and quickened affections yourselves,' Doolittle urges the master of the family.[6] 'Take heed of customariness and formalities,' he warns.[7] Proper motive, attitude, and goal are crucial.

Frequency, Length and Tone

This raises the issue of frequency. Without exception, all of the older champions of family worship urge twice daily, morning and evening family worship. They base their argument for morning and evening family worship on the pattern of the temple sacrifices (e.g. Exod. 30:7). David prays at the time of the evening sacrifice in Psalm 141:2, and in the morning in Psalm 5 (cf. Ps. 92:1, 2; see also 2 Tim. 1:3).[8] They point to Daniel's thrice daily prayers (Dan. 6:10), the call to continuous prayer (Luke 18:1; 1 Thess. 5:17; Col. 4:1, 2), the godly widow's prayers

---

3. Ibid.

4. Ibid., IV:369.

5. Ibid.

6. Doolittle, 'Family Prayer,' *Puritan Sermons,* 2:239.

7. Ibid., 251.

8. Also Perkins, *Oeconomie,* 670; Davies, 'Family Religion,' 27; Whitefield, 'Family Religion,' 38; Hamond, *Family Worship,* 109, 110; Baxter, 'Directory,' *Works,* I:422; Newton, 'Family Worship,' *Letters,* 89; Heywood, 'Family Altar,' *Works,* IV:314.

'night and day' (1 Tim. 4:5; cf. Acts 2:37), as well as the Apostle's (1 Thess. 3:10; 2 Tim. 1:3), and other references to morning and evening prayers (Rev. 7:15; Neh. 1:6; Ps. 88:1), morning and evening Scripture study (Ps. 1:2; Josh. 1:8), and morning and evening praises (Ps. 92:1, 2). Baxter makes the point that

> Morning and evening sacrifices were offered to the Lord; and there is at least equal reason that gospel worship should be as frequent ... in gospel times of greater light and holiness, we should not come behind them in times of the law.[9]

Typically the classic authors caution against lengthy devotions. 'Be short and serious,' Heywood counsels.[10] Alexander admits that 'it was the fault of our forefathers to make it insufferably long.'[11] This was not the case with Philip Henry, 'for he was seldom long, and never tedious in the service,' says his biographer. It was his aim 'to make it a pleasure and not a task to his children and servants.'[12] Often, more is less. Davies suggests a quarter or half an hour morning and evening.[13] Henry counsels, 'You need not be long in the service, but you ought to be lively in it.'[14] Family worship should be 'warm and lively,' says Heywood, like the Lord's Prayer, 'expressive and full of

---

9. Baxter, 'Directory,' *Works*, I:422.

10. Heywood, 'Family Altar,' *Works*, IV:397.

11. Alexander, *Family Worship*, 194.

12. Williams, *Philip and Matthew Henry*, 79; 'Be not too short, nor yet too tedious' (Doolittle, 'Family Prayer,' *Puritan Sermons*, 2:242).

13. Davies, 'Family Religion,' 23.

14. Henry, 'Church in the House,' *Works*, I:265 (my emphasis).

Understanding Family Worship

earnestness.'[15] 'Care should be taken,' says Newton, 'that the combined services (of reading, singing, and praying) do not run into an inconvenient length.'[16]

Schedule

One should choose suitable times for family worship. For example, don't leave it for the end of the day. 'It will not be so seasonable to go down upon your knees,' Heywood warns, 'when you are fitter to lie down in your beds.'[17] 'Late prayers are too commonly sleepy prayers,' Doolittle agrees.[18] Most families will find it suitable to schedule family worship in connection with family meals, before family members are too busy or too tired. It is vital that the family be able to 'attend upon the Lord without distraction' (1 Cor. 7:35, KJV). Establish a stated time that the whole family can count on and adjust to, and yet be flexible enough to adapt to unanticipated disruptions.

Finally, establish order in the home. 'Order your families aright,' Heywood urges. Maintain 'due order and government.' Ensure 'that every member in your family know and keep in their posts and places.' Good order, a common Puritan theme, will ensure that family members have time for the accomplishment of all their duties, including family worship.

---

15. Heywood, 'Family Altar,' *Works,* IV:392.

16. Newton, 'Family Worship,' *Letters,* 90; see also Lye, 'Profitable Catechizing,' *Puritan Sermons,* 2:120; Lee, 'Conversion,' *Puritan Sermons,* 1:150.

17. Heywood, 'Family Altar,' *Works,* IV:396.

18. Doolittle, 'Family Prayer,' *Puritan Sermons,* 2:241.

> Let every work know its time and every one know his work, that confusion may not shortcut religion: order facilitates any business, prevents impediments, and produceth good success.[19]

Carving out time for family worship may have a positive impact upon the whole range of family duties. As time for the family's devotional life is accommodated, time-usage more generally is evaluated and higher priorities may be more firmly established.

---

19. Heywood, 'Family Altars,' *Works,* IV:375.

5
Barriers to Family Worship

'There is no truth so plain, no duty so good, but Satan can furnish a witty head and a wicked heart with plausible arguments against it,' Heywood laments.[1] As we've seen, Baxter and others insist that a zealous Christian doesn't need multiple arguments to convince him of the need of family worship. He doesn't need to be persuaded 'to feast his soul with God, and to delight himself in the frequent exercises of faith and love.' To those who still are not convinced and need further proofs, Baxter urges,

> Let them know that if they will open their eyes, and recover their appetites, and feel their sins, and observe their daily wants and dangers, and get but a heart that loveth God, these reasons then will seem sufficient to convince them of so sweet, and profitable, and necessary a work.[2]

---

1. Ibid., IV:328.

2. Baxter, 'Directory,' *Works,* 1:422; Heywood answers twenty objections to family worship! ('Family Altar,' *Works,* IV:328-444).

Understanding Family Worship

What, then, are some of the unworthy excuses that are offered?

Lack of Ability

The older authors commonly attempt to answer objections to family worship such as, 'I have no ability to pray.' Davies won't hear of it. Don't know how to pray? 'If you had a proper sense of your wants, this plea would not hinder you. Did you ever hear a beggar, however ignorant, make this objection? A sense of his necessities is an unfailing fountain of his eloquence.'[3] For Heywood, 'Desire is the soul of prayer.' It is 'by praying, men may learn to pray aright.'[4] More importantly, God looks at the heart, not the form of words. 'It is not parts, and gifts, and florid expressions that God looks at,' says Doolittle, 'but an humble, penitent, broken, and believing heart.'[5]

Similarly, Doddridge maintains,

> Where the heart is rightly disposed, it does not require any uncommon abilities to discharge family worship in a decent and edifying manner.[6]

If one is lacking eloquence, Swinnock answers,

---

3. Davies, 'Family Religion,' 27.

4. Heywood, 'Family Altar,' *Works,* IV:330.

5. Doolittle, 'Family Prayer,' *Puritan Sermons,* 2:263.

6. Doddridge, 'Family Religion,' 68; see also Williams, *Philip and Matthew Henry,* 77: 'God… cares not how little there is of the head in the duty, so there be a great deal of the *heart.*'

> A sanctified heart is better than a silver tongue... Pray much in secret and thou wilt quickly learn to pray well in private.[7]

Besides, there are helps that may be obtained which provide forms of prayer that might be utilized.[8]

LACK OF TIME

The frenetic pace of life in the modern world is proverbial. Many find it difficult to squeeze in time for family worship. Members of the household are coming and going at such a rapid pace that it proves challenging to gather the family for its devotions. What we have urged above, regarding order, is one answer. If we still object that we lack time for family worship, Doddridge and the classic authors 'cut the objection short at once,' asking 'whether you do not have time for many other things, which you know to be of much less importance.' He asks pointedly, 'How many hours in a week do you spend for amusement, while you have none for devotion in your family?'[9] Henry is scathing in his rebuke:

> You can spare no time at all for it in the morning, nor any in the evening, till you are half asleep. It is thrust into a corner, and almost lost in a crowd of worldly business and carnal converse. When it is done, it is done so slightly, in so much haste, and with so little reverence, that it makes no impression upon yourselves

---
7. Swinnock, 'Christian Man's Calling,' *Works,* I:339.
8. See *Family Worship Book,* 26-31, 36-43, 98-107.
9. Doddridge, 'Family Religion,' 67.

or your families. The Bible lies ready, but you have no time to read ... you yourselves can take up with a word or two of prayer, or rest in a lifeless, heartless tale of words. Thus it is every day, and perhaps little better on the Lord's day, –no repetition, no catechizing, no singing of psalms, or none to any purpose. Is it thus with any of your families? Is this the present state of the church in your house? My brethren, 'these things ought not' to be so. It is not enough that you do that which is good, but you must do it well. God and religion have in effect no place in your hearts or houses, if they have not the innermost and the uppermost place. Christ will come no whither to be an underling; he is not a guest to be set behind the door. What comfort, what benefit can you promise to yourselves from such trifling services as these, – from an empty form of godliness without the power of it?[10]

TIRESOME

Others may object that family worship is tedious. They remember how dull, how tiresome participation in family devotions was in their childhood, and are loathe to repeat the ordeal with their children. J.W. Alexander responds, 'Very ignorant, very stupid, or very irreligious people, may transform it into a tedious and burdensome routine.' This is true enough. Yet 'this is not fault of the ordinance.' Where there is inspired leadership, family worship may be made daily 'a

---

10. Henry, 'Church in the House,' *Works,* I:265; see also Doolittle, 'Family Prayer,' *Puritan Sermons,* 2:265-270; Davies, 'Family Religion,' 26; Doddridge, 'Family Religion,' 67-68; Alexander, *Family Worship,* 54ff; Heywood, 'Family Worship,' *Works,* IV:313; 406.

delightful and animating means of grace,' on which 'shines with a pure and hallowed attraction.'[11]

We have noted the concern of the older authors that the duty of family worship not become a formality. That which is conscientiously performed may come to be 'mechanically performed,' Newton warns, 'unless we are continually looking to the Lord to keep our hearts alive.' The master of the family should be 'lively and earnest in performance of the duty,' he urges, 'and likewise circumspect and consistent in every part of his behavior at other times.'[12]

Alexander insists that 'every part of it should be solemn, and fitted to repress all levity.' Care should be taken that 'every secular task or amusement be suspended and absolute silence and quiet be enforced.' He commends simplicity in speech yet also 'a holy animation, as that which will arrest attention, and make way for pleasant memories.'[13]

These are but a few of the many excuses that might be offered for the neglect of family worship. Recognize them for what they are: excuses to which every family may be tempted to succumb and which must be overcome. Pick a time to gather the family and stick to it. Be as disciplined about family worship as one is about matters of hygiene and grooming. A lifetime of daily family Bible reading, prayer, and the singing of praises cannot but pay spiritual dividends.

---

11. Alexander, *Family Worship*, 248-249.
12. Newton, 'Family Worship,' *Letters,* 90.
13. Alexander, *Family Worship*, 194-195.

6

Catechizing

We include catechizing in our survey of family worship because the family devotional hour often will prove the most advantageous time to instruct children in the things of God. A few minutes of recitation in the context of family worship may go a long way in transmitting parental faith to covenant children.

A sketch of the history of catechetical instruction may be found in the present author's *Catechizing Our Children*.[1] Luke wrote to Theophilus regarding the things he had been 'taught' (*katēcheō*), from which we get our word 'catechize' (Luke 1:4). The Apostle Paul refers to the one who is 'taught' sharing all good things with the one who 'teaches,' or the one who is catechized sharing with the one who catechizes (both are forms of the verb *katēcheō*) (Gal. 6:6; cf. Rom. 2:18; Acts 18:25; 1 Cor. 14:19). He also speaks of 'a form of teaching' (Rom. 6:17) and 'a form of sound words' (2 Tim. 1:13). The question and answer format goes back to Socrates (d. 399 B.C.) and

---

1. T. L. Johnson, *Catechizing Our Children* (Edinburgh: The Banner of Truth Trust, 2013), 7-15; also *Family Worship Book,* 61-91.

the ancient Greeks. It was adapted by the early Christians such as Cyprian (199-258) and Origen (c. 184-c.253), and examples of which include Cyril of Jerusalem's *Catechetical Lectures* (c. 350), Clement of Alexandria's *Pegagorgus* (c. 198), Lactantius' *Institutes* (c. 303-311), Athanasius *Synopsis*, Augustine's *On the Catechizing of the Uninstructed* (c. 400), and *Enchiridion*. Catechizing flourished in the patristic era, waned in the Middle Ages, and was revived by the Reformers, beginning with Luther as early as 1516-17. His *Small Catechism* (1529) was among his most successful publications, doing much to popularize Protestant doctrine. A number of Reformers followed suit, the most important being Calvin's Genevan Catechism, first published in 1537 and revised in 1542 and again in 1545, followed by the *Heidelberg Catechism* of 1563, the standard for the Dutch and German Reformed churches.

Thomas Cranmer provided a catechism for the Church of England in the first *Book of Common Prayer* (1549). However, by far the most important catechism in the English-speaking world has been the Westminster Assembly's *Shorter Catechism*, first published in 1648, quickly adopted by the Presbyterian Church of Scotland, and widely utilized by Presbyterians, Baptists, and Congregationalists worldwide. *The Catechism for Young Children* came later (1840) as a popular supplement or preparation for the *Shorter Catechism*.[2]

---

2. *Catechism for Young Children, Being an Introduction to the Shorter Catechism* (Philadelphia: Presbyterian Board of Publication and Sabbath-School Work, 1840). Also available in *Family Worship Book*, 61-75.

Catechizing

Parents who wish to lead their children to sincere commitment to Christ should not neglect this proven tool. Thomas Manton (1620-1677) recommends 'with the greatest earnestness the work of catechizing.'[3] According to Whitefield, citing Genesis 18:17, Deuteronomy 6:6, 7, and Ephesians 6:1, 2, 'scarcely any thing is more frequently pressed upon us in the holy writ than this duty of catechizing.'[4] Reformed luminaries from Calvin to the Westminster Assembly, to Richard Baxter (1615-1691) to John Owen (1616-1683) to Thomas Watson (1620-1686) to John Flavel (1627-1691) to Philip Doddridge (1702-1751) to Charles Hodge (1797-1878) to B. B. Warfield (1851-1921) to John Murray (1898-1975) enthusiastically endorsed the catechizing of children. Many of the Puritans wrote their own catechisms or wrote supplements of the *Shorter Catechism*. Matthew Henry (1662-1714), we are not surprised to discover, not only provides the best argument for family worship, but also the most persuasive argument for catechizing in his 'Sermon Concerning the Catechizing of Youth.'[5] This sermon is an exposition of 2 Timothy 1:13.

---

3. Manton, 'Epistle,' 8.

4. Whitefield, 'Family Religion,' 39; see also Gouge, *Domestical Duties*, 287, 394-395; Lye, 'Profitable Catechizing,' *Puritan Sermons*, 2:101; 105-108; 112, 115.

5. Henry, 'Sermon Concerning the Catechizing of Youth,' *The Complete Works of Matthew Henry: Treatises, Sermons, and Tracks*, Volumes I-II (1855; Grand Rapids: Baker Book House, 1979), II:157-173.

> Follow the pattern of the sound words that you have heard from me, in the faith and love that are in Christ Jesus (2 Tim 1:13).

He argues that the 'form' (NASB, KJV) or 'pattern of sound words' of which the Apostle Paul speaks are the doctrines which comprise 'the main principles of Christianity.' However, these principles 'lie scattered in the Scripture' and must be 'collected and brought together' if we are rightly to understand them and believe them. This is what our catechisms and confessions do. They 'pick up from the various parts of holy writ those passages which ... contain the essentials of religion, the foundations and main pillars upon which Christianity is built.' These 'truths of God' are then 'arranged and put in order' so that one might easily see 'how one thing tends to another, and all centre in Christ, and the glory of God in Christ.' The whole, then, is 'brought down to the capacity of young ones.'[6] It is a time-tested method of passing on one's faith to one's children. 'It is,' Henry insists, 'a very great advantage to young people, to hear and learn the Christian forms of sound words in the days of their youth; to have been well taught some good catechism, or confession of faith.'[7] He urges, 'Let families be well catechized, and then the public preaching of the word will be the more profitable, and the more successful.'[8]

Baxter provides twenty-five directions for families in their catechetical instruction. We will not list them

---
6. Ibid., II:160-161.

7. Ibid., II:158.

8. Henry, 'Church in the House,' *Works,* I:262.

all, though all are worthy of careful consideration. Instead we will summarize most of what he commends, supplemented by the insights of others.

BEGIN EARLY

Begin the work of memorization early. 'Cause your younger children to learn the words, though they be not yet capable of understanding the matter,' Baxter advises.[9] Don't make the mistake of thinking that one makes hypocrites of one's children if one teaches them the words of Scripture or the catechism before they have understanding. Instead he points out the advantage that comes later:

> when they come to years of understanding, that part of their work is done, and they have nothing to do but to study the meaning and use of those words which they have learned already.[10]

Lye points out that all learning progresses from parroting to understanding. Children are taught to memorize their a-b-c's, vowels, numbers, vocabulary, and even names and dates before they come to comprehend their meaning. Understanding grows with time. Begin 'as soon as ever their understandings begin to bud and blossom,' Lye advises.[11] In addition, there are advantages to beginning early before their minds have been poisoned by error. 'It is best growing a fair picture on a rasa tabula,' says Lye.

---

9. Baxter, 'Christian Directory,' *Works,* 1:479.
10. Ibid.
11. See Lye, 'Profitable Catechizing,' *Puritan Sermons,* 2:113.

Understanding Family Worship

'Little ones have not as yet imbibed such false principles and notions, nor are they drenched with such evil habits, as elder ones are too, too frequently dyed with.'[12] If parents begin early to catechize their children, they may teach them directly without having first to root up error.

PRE-CATECHISM

Prior to formal catechizing, pre-catechtical instruction may take place on an informal basis, as follows:

1. Begin by explaining rudimentary truths: that there is a God who has made them and all things, who is to be honored and worshiped, that life is brief and uncertain, that judgment awaits in eternity. The opening questions of the *Catechism for Young Children* may be helpful to this end: 'Who made you? God'; 'What else did God make? God made all things'; etc.[13]

2. Utilize simple illustrations and metaphors. Witnessing a beautiful sunrise or sunset, a beautiful landscape or seascape? Speak of God's creative skill. Eating an especially delicious orange or strawberry, apple or pineapple? Speak of God's goodness. Enduring a powerful storm, lightning, thunder, howling winds, powerful tides? Speak of God's power. Dressing your child? Speak of being clothed with Christ's righteousness. Walking into your house? Speak of that house made without hands that we one day will have in heaven (2 Cor. 5:1). Standing by a riverside? Speak of the living waters that are ours in Christ (John 4). 'Teach those

---

12. Ibid., 117; so also Gouge, *Domestical Duties,* 398.
13. See also *Family Worship Book,* 61-75.

little bees to suck spiritual honey out of every flower,' says Lye.[14]

3. Teach them the most memorable of Bible stories: the fall, Noah and the ark, Lot and Sodom, Joseph, the exodus, the golden calf, Gideon, Samson, David and Goliath, Daniel and the lions' den, the three children in the fiery furnace, Jonah and the fish, and so on. The Bible is full of memorable stories, parables, and events. Use them.

4. Introduce them to the basic elements of worship through family worship: prayer, singing praises, and reading Scripture. Doing so has the added advantage of preparing the children for participation in public worship. In this way, family worship and public worship reinforce each other.

5. Bring them to public services 'as soon as they can come to be there, without the disturbance of the church,' advises Lye.[15] The assembly of Israel regularly included the 'little ones' (Deut. 29:11; Josh. 8:35; Isa. 2:5; Joel 2:16; Jonah 3:5). Jesus welcomed the little children and blessed them (Matt. 19:13-15; Mark 10:13; Luke 18:15). While much that takes place in public worship will be beyond their grasp, there is profit in simply being there, seeing mother and father, seeing families, seeing young and old engaged in the worship of God.

6. Include what the older sources called 'godly conferences' in which the children's understanding is explored (cf. Matt. 13:5; Mark 4:34). There is no replacing actual conversations with one's children regarding the

---

14. Lye, 'Profitable Catechizing,' *Puritan Sermons,* 2:118.
15. Ibid.

Understanding Family Worship

things of God. Ironically, sadly, this rather obvious practice is neglected by parents to the detriment of their children.

CATECHISMS

As for catechizing proper, Baxter advises that parents adopt the following order which, over 350-odd years later still seems sound and wise:

1. Have them memorize and learn the Creed, the Lord's Prayer, and the Ten Commandments as summaries of what we must believe, what we must desire and seek, and what we must practice. These three forms have been a part of catechetical instruction at least since Augustine. These also are what are called 'fixed forms' in traditional churches, recited in weekly services. Memorizing these early facilitates the participation of children in public worship.

2. Have them memorize and learn a short catechism, and then later the larger catechism. Baxter reckons that 'the shorter and larger catechisms of the (Westminster) Assembly are very well fitted to this use.'[16] Lye commends their 'peculiar excellency' in that 'every answer in them is an entire proposition itself, without relation to the question preceding.'[17] Given what seems to be a diminishing capacity for memorization in our electronic age, the *Larger Catechism* may be a bridge too far. A more

---

16. Baxter, 'Christian Directory,' *Works,* 1:479; also Manton quotes Baxter in his preface to the Westminster Standards: 'First, let them read and learn the Shorter Catechism, and next the Larger, and lastly, read the Confession of Faith' ('Mr. Manton's Epistle to the Reader' in *Westminster Confession of Faith,* 12); Lye, 'Profitable Catechizing,' *Puritan Sermons,* 2:121.

17. Lye, 'Profitable Catechizing,' *Puritan Sermons,* 2:121.

practical suggestion is to utilize the *Catechism for Young Children* and the *Shorter Catechism*. By any standard, memorization of the *Longer Catechism* is a daunting task.

3. Read to them good expositions of the catechisms (which recall, cover the Creed generally and the Ten Commandments, and Lord's Prayer specifically). Thomas Watson's *A Body of Divinity* (which originally included what are now separate volumes on the Ten Commandments and the Lord's Prayer) is the kind of book Baxter is recommending.[18] G. I. Williamson's more recent exposition of the *Shorter Catechism* is deep, accessible, and useful.[19]

4. In all family instruction, Baxter advises that parents be sure to 'let it be always with such a mixture of familiarity and seriousness that may carry along their serious attentions, whether they will or no. Speak to them as if they or you were dying, and as if you saw God, and heaven, and hell.'[20]

5. Explain baptism and the covenant of grace.[21] In other words, explain the whole plan of salvation, from the problem of the human condition to the covenant of salvation in Christ. Explain, says Baxter,

---

18. See also Lye, 'Profitable Catechizing,' *Puritan Sermons*, 2:123. He commends expositions of the *Shorter Catechism* by Alleyn, Vincent, and Doolittle.

19. G. I. Williamson, *The Westminster Shorter Catechism: For Study Classes* (1970; Phillipsburg, NJ: P & R Publishing, 2003).

20. Baxter, 'Christian Directory,' *Works*, 1:

21. Gouge urges that one utilize the public ordinances such as baptism and the Lord's Supper as teaching tools (*Domestical Duties*, 395).

Understanding Family Worship

> that he that consenteth unfeignedly to this covenant, is a member of Christ, a justified, reconciled child of God, and an heir of heaven, and so continuing, shall be saved; and he that doth not shall be damned. This is the covenant, that in baptism we solemnly entered into with God the Father, Son, and Holy Ghost, as our Father and Felicity, our Saviour, and our Sanctifier.[22]

Regularly remind the children that they belong to God, that the mark of Christ is upon them through baptism, and even when they stray, even when they contemplate rebellion, nevertheless they are His and He will not let them go.

Further Advice to Parents

Baxter and Lye offer additional coaching for parents in connection with the manner of catechizing.

1. Baxter urges direct, personal questions and application with one's children, in addition to catechizing. His extended counsel is worth quoting at length.

> Take each of them sometimes by themselves, and there describe to them the work of renovation, and ask them, whether ever such a work was wrought upon them. Show them the true marks of grace, and help them to try themselves; urge them to tell you truly, whether their love to God or the creature, to heaven or earth, to holiness or flesh-pleasing, be more; and what is that hath their hearts, and care, and chief endeavor: and if you find them regenerate, help to strengthen them; if you find them too much dejected, help to comfort

---

22. Baxter, 'Christian Directory,' *Works*, I:482.

them; and if you find them unregenerate, help to convince them, and then to humble them, and then to show them the remedy in Christ, and then show them their duty that they may have part in Christ, and drive all home to the end that you desire to see; but do all this with love, and gentleness, and privacy.

Baxter encourages a methodology featuring thorough questioning:

> Some pertinent questions which by the answer will engage them to teach themselves, or to judge themselves, will be sometimes of very great use. As such as these; 'Do you not know that you must shortly die? Do you not believe that immediately your souls must enter upon an endless life of joy or misery? Will worldly wealth and honours, or fleshly pleasures, be pleasant to you then? Had you then rather be a saint, or an ungodly sinner? Had you not then rather be one of the holiest that the world despised and abused, than one of the greatest and richest of the wicked? When time is past, and you must give account of it, had you not then rather it had been spent in holiness, and obedience, and diligent preparation for the life to come, than in pride, and pleasure, and pampering the flesh? How could you make shift to forget your endless life so long? or to sleep quietly in an unregenerate state? What if you had died before conversion, what think you had become of you, and where had you now been? Do you think that any of those in hell are glad that they were ungodly? Or have now any pleasure in their former merriments and sin? What think you would they do, if it were all to do

again? ... such kind of questions urge the conscience, and much convince.[23]

Baxter's ideal of thoroughness may be difficult to replicate. Yet his overall point is well-taken. By drawing out answers from one's children, one attains a clearer insight into their level of understanding as well as leading them logically step by step to the conclusions one hopes they will reach.

2. Baxter cautions not to attempt to do too much:

> Tire them not out with too much at once; but give it them as they can receive it. Narrow-mouthed bottles must not be filled as wider vessels.[24] Babies must be fed with a spoon. Plants can be ruined by too much watering. The little ones must be driven gently (Gen. 33:13).

Lye agrees: 'Avoid all tedious prolixity,' he urges.[25] For this reason we have counseled in the *Family Worship Book* that one limit the family's devotional time to 10-15 minutes. This length is both achievable and bearable. Similarly, a mere five minutes a day consistently maintained is sufficient to master both the *Catechism for Young Children* and the *Shorter Catechism*.

3. Lye urges parents not to become discouraged by the resistance to catechizing they encounter from their children. Their 'averseness ... is not the least argument

---

23. Ibid., 1:482.
24. Ibid.
25. Lye, 'Profitable Catechizing,' *Puritan Sermons,* 2:120.

of its singular usefulness,' he argues counterintuitively.[26] As with the case with painful medical procedures, the patient may complain, or resist, yet his discomfort is no argument against the treatment. So it is with catechizing. Five minutes a day is not a hardship. Ignore the whining.

4. Parents should not be discouraged by a lack of tangible success from their labors. Lye cites a timeless principle: we are called to be faithful, not successful. 'God takes the measure of his servants, not from their success, which is his soul work; but from their sedulous and faithful endeavors, which is their duty.'[27] Faithful parents are playing what might be called the 'long game.' Results may not be immediate, yet we trust that fruit will eventually be forthcoming. More on this in a moment.

5. Baxter wisely urges a positive teaching environment.

> Labour to make all sweet and pleasant to them ... entice them with kindnesses and rewards. Be kind to your children when they do well... A small gift now and then, might signify much to the further benefit of their souls.[28]

'Labour in to insinuate yourselves into their affections,' says Lye.[29]

---

26. Ibid., 2:124.
27. Ibid; sedulous: sharing dedication and diligence.
28. Baxter, 'Christian Directory,' *Works,* 1:482.
29. Lye, 'Profitable Catechizing,' *Puritan Sermons,* 2:125.

6. Finally, if any say this is too much, Baxter counters,

> I entreat them to consult with Christ that died for them, whether souls be not precious, and worth all this ado? And to consider how small a labour all this is, in comparison of the everlasting end; and to remember, that all is gain and pleasure, and a delight to those that have holy hearts; and to remember, that the effects to the church and kingdom, of such holy government of families, would quite over-compensate all the pains.[30]

'Happy is the family where the worship of God is constantly and conscientiously maintained,' says Newton.[31] Let us then maintain, as Heywood urges, this 'most indisputable duty.'[32]

---

30. Ibid.
31. Newton, 'Family Worship,' *Letters,* 92.
32. Heywood, 'Family Altar,' *Works,* IV:363.

7
Parental Hopes

Can we expect good results from our labors as parents? Indeed. Is this not the promise of Genesis 17:7? Will not our God be our God and our children's? Does He not promise to be such? Is not the gospel promise for us and for our children (Acts 2:39)? Shall 'posterity' not serve Him? Shall not the 'coming generation' be 'told of the Lord' and shall they not 'proclaim his righteousness to a people yet unborn' (Ps. 22:30, 31 cf. 71:18; Joel 1:3)? Has God not promised,

> For I will pour water on the thirsty land, and streams on the dry ground; I will pour my Spirit upon your offspring, and my blessing on your descendants. They shall spring up among the grass like willows by flowing streams. This one will say, 'I am the Lord's,' another will call on the name of Jacob, and another will write on his hand, 'The Lord's,' and name himself by the name of Israel' (Isa. 44:3-5).

Is it for God's 'blessing on (our) descendants' for which we labor in our family worship and catechizing? 'There is none in the world so likely as you to be instruments of their eternal good,' John Flavel assures parents in his classic *The Mystery of Providence*.[1]

Hildersham is not concerned that children may not understand the catechism or Scripture lessons. Understanding will come later, as it did with Jesus' disciples, as John tells us (John 2:22; 12:16). With understanding will come the good that accompanies understanding. Moreover, parents should be encouraged. Proverbs 22:6 promises that 'when he is old he will not depart from it,' that is, from 'the way he should go.' 'The wise man assure us,' says Doddridge, 'that we may reasonably expect the most happy consequence from it.' What about the old saying, Many a young saint was proved to be an old devil? Hildersham also cites Proverbs 22:6, now comparing a young child to a vessel that long retains the savor of the liquid with which it is first seasoned.[2] Doddridge, continuing in his expositions of Proverbs 22:6 speaks of the parental training of children having a 'fair probability' of succeeding, given that it is both 'a very rational method,' and 'a method which He has crowned with singular success.'[3]

What can be said to Christian parents who see no fruit from their labors to instruct their children? Swinnock recognizes that the benefits of a Christian education may be delayed:

---

1. John Flavel, *The Mystery of Providence* (1678; Edinburgh: The Banner of Truth Trust, 1976), 58.
2. Hildersham, 'Disciplining Children,' 130-131.
3. Doddridge, 'Religious Education,' 197-198, cf.183-184.

Parental Hopes

> Their pious education may be profitable, though not presently. The good seed thou now sowest, may yield a blessed crop, though a nipping winter should come between; however, thou hast delivered thy own soul; the master hath his quarterage, whether his scholar learn or loiter, and the physician hath his fee, whether the patient recover or die.[4]

There is no infallible line between parental faithfulness in family worship and the salvation of the children. Prodigal children emerge from the godliest families and the godliest churches. Yet we do have the promises of God which we must claim and of which we must remind God when we pray. William Grimshaw (1708-1763), minister of the Church of England in Haworth, Yorkshire, was an associate of the Wesleys and Whitefield during the years of the Great Awakening and a powerful preacher in his own right. What had been described as a desolate parish grew from 12 to 1200 members under his pastorate. Yet he left this world not seeing the fulfillment of the covenant promises of God in connection with his only son, John, twenty-seven years old at the time of his father's death. John was 'a waster and drunkard,' according to Grimshaw's biographer, who 'brought untold distress to his father.'[5] However afterwards, 'never having forgotten his father's advice and example,' says J. C. Ryle, John did come to saving knowledge of Christ. Dying just three

---

4. Swinnock, 'Christian Man's Calling,' *Works,* I:403.
5. Faith Cook, *William Grimshaw of Haworth* (Edinburgh: The Banner of Truth Trust, 1997), 291.

years after his father, John's last words were, 'What will my old father say when he sees me in heaven?'[6]

Ordinarily, faithful Christian parents can be confident that their children will come to faith in Christ. Consistent church attendance and family worship will bear fruit in the lives of children reared in such homes. The promises of God will be fulfilled, though according to God's timetable, not ours. Henry encourages us:

> If you make conscience of doing your duty, by keeping up family doctrine, —if you teach them the good and the right way, and warn them of by-paths, —if you reprove, exhort, and encourage them as there is occasion, —if you pray with them, and for them, and set them a good example, and at last consult their soul's welfare in the disposal of them, you have done your part, and may comfortably leave the issue and success with God.

Again, he says,

> God will be with you in a way of mercy while you are with him in a way of duty.[7]

---

6. J. C. Ryle, *Holiness: Its Nature, Hindrances, Difficulties, and Roots* (1877, 1879; Edinburgh: The Banner of Truth Trust, 2014), 367.

7. Henry, 'Church in the House,' Works, I:254, 259.

Bibliography

Alexander, James W. *Thoughts on Family Worship*. Morgan, PA: Soli Deo Gloria Publications, 1990.

Bainton, Roland H. *Here I Stand: A Life of Martin Luther.* 1950; Nashville: Abingdon Press, 1978.

Baxter, Richard. 'A Christian Directory,' *The Practical Works of Richard Baxter,* Volume 1. 1654-5, 1673; Ligonier, PA: Soli Deo Publications, 19th century reprint, 1990.

_____. 'The Poor Man's Family Book,' T*he Practical Works of Richard Baxter,* Volume IV. 1654-5, 1673; Ligonier, PA: Soli Deo Gloria Publications, 19th century reprint, 1990.

Calvin, John. *The First Epistle of Paul the Apostle to the Corinthians*, translator John. W. Fraser, Calvin's Commentaries 1546, 1547. Grand Rapids: Wm. B. Eerdmans Publishing Co., 1960.

Catechism for Young Children, Being an Introduction to the Shorter Catechism. (Philadelphia: Presbyterian Board of Publication and Sabbath-School Work, 1840.

Catholic Household Blessings and Prayers. Washington, DC: United States Catholic Conference, 1988.

Cook, Faith. *William Grimshaw of Hayworth* Edinburgh: The Banner of Truth Trust, 1997.

Davies, Horton. *The Worship of the English Puritans*. 1948; Morgan, PA: Soli Deo Gloria Publications, 1997.

Davies, Samuel, 'The Necessity and Excellency of Family Religion,' *The Godly Family: A Series of Essays on the Duties of Parents and Children*. Morgan, PA: Soli Deo Gloria Publications, 1993.

Doddridge, Philip. 'A Plain and Serious Address on the Important Subject of Family Religion,' *The Godly Family: A Series of Essays on the Duties of Parents and Children*. Morgan, PA: Soli Deo Gloria Publications, 1993.

_____. 'Four Sermons on the Religious Education of Children,' in Kistler (ed.), *The Godly Family: A Series of Essays on the Duties of Parents and Children*. Morgan, PA: Soli Deo Gloria Publications, 1993.

Doolittle, Thomas. 'How May the Duty of Daily Family Prayer Be Best Managed for the Spiritual Benefit of Every One in the Family,' *Puritan Sermons*, 1659-1689. 1844; Wheaton: Richard Owen Roberts, 1981.

Edwards, Jonathan. 'Memoirs of Jonathan Edwards,' in *The Works of Jonathan Edwards*, Vol. 1. 1834; Edinburgh: The Banner of Truth Trust, 1974.

Gouge, William. *Of Domestical Duties*. 1622; Pensacola, FL: Puritan Reprints, 2006.

Gurnall, William. *The Christian in Complete Armour*. 1662 and 1665; Edinburgh: The Banner of Truth Trust, 1964.

Hamond, George. *The Case for Family Worship*. 1694; Orlando, FL: Soli Deo Gloria Publications, 2005.

Bibliography

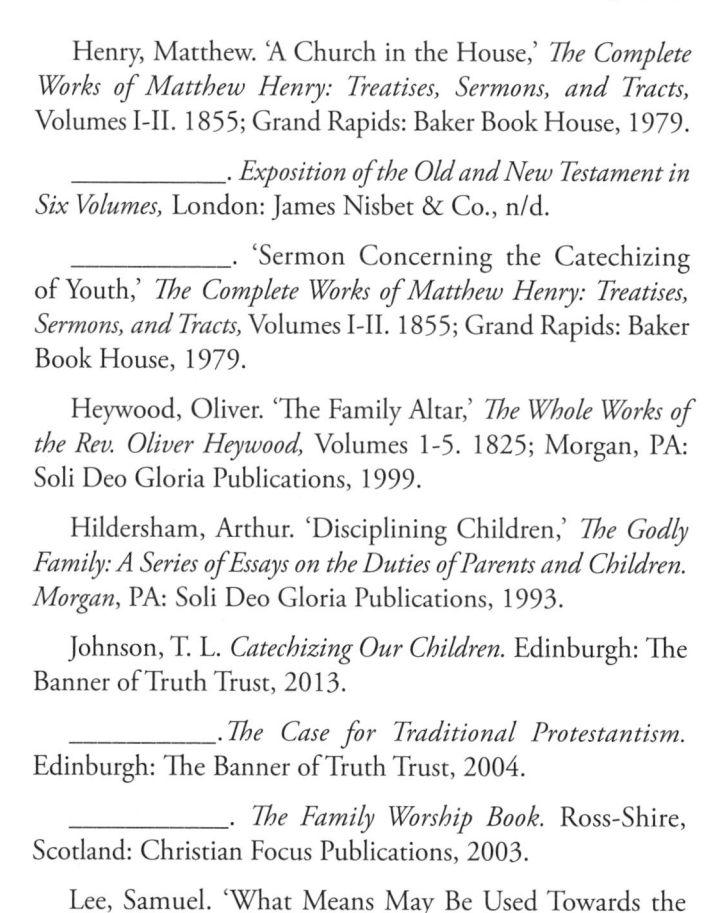

Henry, Matthew. 'A Church in the House,' *The Complete Works of Matthew Henry: Treatises, Sermons, and Tracts,* Volumes I-II. 1855; Grand Rapids: Baker Book House, 1979.

_____. *Exposition of the Old and New Testament in Six Volumes,* London: James Nisbet & Co., n/d.

_____. 'Sermon Concerning the Catechizing of Youth,' *The Complete Works of Matthew Henry: Treatises, Sermons, and Tracts,* Volumes I-II. 1855; Grand Rapids: Baker Book House, 1979.

Heywood, Oliver. 'The Family Altar,' *The Whole Works of the Rev. Oliver Heywood,* Volumes 1-5. 1825; Morgan, PA: Soli Deo Gloria Publications, 1999.

Hildersham, Arthur. 'Disciplining Children,' *The Godly Family: A Series of Essays on the Duties of Parents and Children.* Morgan, PA: Soli Deo Gloria Publications, 1993.

Johnson, T. L. *Catechizing Our Children.* Edinburgh: The Banner of Truth Trust, 2013.

_____. *The Case for Traditional Protestantism.* Edinburgh: The Banner of Truth Trust, 2004.

_____. *The Family Worship Book.* Ross-Shire, Scotland: Christian Focus Publications, 2003.

Lee, Samuel. 'What Means May Be Used Towards the Conversion of Our Carnal Relations,' in *Puritan Sermons, 1659-1689.* 1844; Wheaton: Richard Owen Roberts, 1981.

'Little Churches: Ritual in the Home,' *The Journal of the Liturgical Conference: Liturgy,* Vol, 21, Nov. 4, 2006.

Lye, Thomas. 'By What Scriptural Rules May Catechizing Be So Managed as That It May Become Most Universally Profitable,' in *Puritan Sermons, 1659-1689.* 1844; Wheaton: Richard Owen Roberts, 1981.

Manton, Thomas. 'Mr. Thomas Manton's Epistle to the Reader,' *Westminster Confession of Faith*. Inverness: Free Presbyterian Publications, 1983.

M'Cheyne, Robert Murray. 'Family Government,' *Additional Remains of the Rev. Robert Murray M'Cheyne*. Edinburgh: Johnstone and Hunter, 1984.

McKee, Elsie Anne (ed.). J*ohn Calvin: Writings on Pastoral Piety*. New York: Paulist Press, 2010.

Newton, John. 'Family Worship,' *The Letters of John Newton*. London: The Banner of Truth Trust, 1965.

Old, Hughes O. 'Matthew Henry and the Puritan Discipline of Family Prayer,' in John Leith (ed.), *Calvin Studies,* VII, 'Papers Presented at a Colloquium on Calvin Studies,' Davidson College Presbyterian Church, Davidson, NC, Jan. 28-29, 1994.

Ozment, Steven. *Protestants: The Birth of a Revolution*. New York: Doubleday, 1992.

_____. *When Fathers Ruled: Family Life in Reformation Europe*. Cambridge, MA: Harvard University Press, 1983.

Packer, J. I. *A Quest for Godliness: The Puritan Vision of the Christian Life*. Wheaton, IL: Crossway Books, 1990.

Palmer, Benjamin M. *The Family in its Civil and Churchly Aspects*. 1876; Harrisonburg, VA: Sprinkle Publications, 1981.

Perkins, William. *Oeconomic, or Household Government:* A Short Survey of the Right Manner of Erecting and Ordering a Family, according to the Scriptures. 1609: London: John Haviland, 1631.

Bibliography

Poole, Matthew, *A Commentary on the Whole Bible,* Volumes I-III. 1683-85, 1865; Edinburgh: The Banner of Truth Trust, 1963.

Ryle, J.C. *The Duties of Parents.* Sand Springs, OH: Grace and Truth Books, 2002; first published in *The Upper Room: Being Truth for the Times.* London: William Hunt & Co., 1888.

Safley, Thomas Max. 'Family,' in Hans J. Hillerbrand (ed.), *The Oxford Encyclopedia of the Reformation,* Volumes 1-4. New York: Oxford University Press, 1996.

Swinnock, George. 'The Christian Man's Calling,' *The Works of George Swinnock*, Vol. I. 1808; Edinburgh: The Banner of Truth Trust, 1992.

The Book of Church Order, Presbyterian Church in America.

Trapp, John. *A Commentary on the Old and New Testaments,* Volumes I-V. 1647, 1865-68; Eureka, CA: Tansky Publications, 1997.

Westminster Confession of Faith. Glasgow: Free Presbyterian Publications, 1994.

Whitefield, George. 'The Great Duty of Family Religion,' in Kistler (ed.), *The Godly Family.* Morgan, PA: Soli Deo Gloria Publications, 1993.

Williams, J. B. *The Lives of Philip and Matthew Henry,* 2 Volumes in one. 1698, 1828. Edinburgh: The Banner of Truth Trust, 1974.

Williamson, G. I. *The Westminster Shorter Catechism: For Study Classes.* 1970; Phillipsburg, NJ: P & R Publishing, 2003.

Christian Focus Publications

Our mission statement –

STAYING FAITHFUL

In dependence upon God we seek to impact the world through literature faithful to His infallible Word, the Bible. Our aim is to ensure that the Lord Jesus Christ is presented as the only hope to obtain forgiveness of sin, live a useful life and look forward to heaven with Him.

Our Books are published in four imprints:

CHRISTIAN FOCUS

popular works including biographies, commentaries, basic doctrine and Christian living.

CHRISTIAN HERITAGE

books representing some of the best material from the rich heritage of the church.

MENTOR

books written at a level suitable for Bible College and seminary students, pastors, and other serious readers. The imprint includes commentaries, doctrinal studies, examination of current issues and church history.

CF4•K

children's books for quality Bible teaching and for all age groups: Sunday school curriculum, puzzle and activity books; personal and family devotional titles, biographies and inspirational stories – because you are never too young to know Jesus!

Christian Focus Publications Ltd,
Geanies House, Fearn, Ross-shire,
IV20 1TW, Scotland, United Kingdom.
www.christianfocus.com